SPECKS

AND

PLANKS

SPECKS

AND

PLANKS

STORIES OF HOPE, HUMILITY AND HUMANITY

JEFF LUCAS

WAVERLEY ABBEY
RESOURCES

Published 2020 by CWR, Waverley Abbey House, Waverley Lane, Farnham, Surrey GU9 8EP, UK. Registered Charity No. 294387. Registered limited company No. 1990308.
The right of Jeff Lucas to be identified as the author of this work has been asserted by him in accordance with the Copyright, Designs and Patents Act 1988.

For a list of National Distributors, visit waverleyabbeyresources.org.uk/distributors
Unless otherwise indicated, all Scripture references are from the Holy Bible, New International Version® Anglicised, NIV® Copyright © 1979, 1984, 2011 by Biblica, Inc.® Used by permission. All rights reserved worldwide.

Scripture quotations marked NLT are taken from the *Holy Bible*, New Living Translation, copyright © 1996, 2004, 2015 by Tyndale House Foundation. Used by permission of Tyndale House Publishers Inc., Carol Stream, Illinois 60188. All rights reserved.

Scripture quotations marked *The Message* are taken from THE MESSAGE, copyright © 1993, 2002, 2018 by Eugene H. Peterson. Used by permission of NavPress. All rights reserved. Represented by Tyndale House Publishers, Inc.

Scripture quotations marked NKJV are taken from the New King James Version®. Copyright © 1982 by Thomas Nelson. Used by permission. All rights reserved.

Every effort has been made to ensure that this book contains the correct permissions and references, but if anything has been inadvertently overlooked, the Publisher will be pleased to make the necessary arrangements at the first opportunity. Please contact the Publisher directly.

Concept development, editing, design and production by CWR.
Cover image: Adobe Stock/ oscar0
Printed in the UK by Linneys
ISBN: 978-1-78951-244-1

To Dana, with much love.
What a joy and a gift you are in our family.

This book was written during the early days of the coronavirus pandemic and lockdown when I spent a lot of time in isolation with my ever-loving wife, Kay. I'd like to thank her for not taking my life during that season.

My thanks to the editor of *Premier Christianity* magazine, Sam Hailes, where some of these pieces – now revised and extended – first appeared. Then there's the team at Waverley Abbey Resources – Lynette Brooks, Andrea Bodle and others. I usually compliment the team there for acting nicely and kindly, as good Christians should. I repeat that compliment here because they keep on acting nicely and kindly, and I'm certainly grateful.

Contents

Introduction

This book was written during the peak of the coronavirus pandemic and the worldwide unrest that followed the tragic killing of George Floyd. Many people were becoming weary of the weeks and then months of lockdown and restrictions. Granted, there were many beautiful, sunshine moments shared; there were countless acts of generosity and self-sacrifice. We felt a sense of solidarity as we applauded the NHS, carers and key workers. Ironically, in social distancing, neighbours discovered neighbours. Captain Tom was celebrated not just because of his phenomenal fundraising effort that generated millions of pounds but because of his kindly, warm, humble smile. But there was rage too as we witnessed the nearly nine-minute suffering and death of Mr Floyd in Minnesota. And anger is appropriate when we see flagrant abuses of power. God is angry at injustice.

When I was at Bible college (I think Queen Victoria was on the throne), I was taught the doctrine of immutability, the notion that, as it says in a letter to Phillip Johnson, 'God has no desires and no affections, no true delight or grief, and certainly no sorrow over anything that comes to pass—because His mind is pure, sovereign, irresistible will.'[1] Without wanting to sound too much like Victor Meldrew (remember him?), I don't believe it. The cross of calvary, often described as the Passion, is the result of a God who is passionate about His world and every single person in it.

The God of the Bible, while not dominated in any way by emotion, is emotional. He agonised over the people of Israel and suffered with their suffering. Hosea prophesied about a God whose 'heart churns within' Him over His people (Hos. 11:8, NKJV). He is likened to a husband who is cheated on by his wife (Israel) but loves her still (Hos. 3:1). God is portrayed as a compassionate mother (Isa. 49:15–16) and as an ecstatic father of a wayward son (Luke 15:11–32). At various times He is said to be grieved, angry, pleased, joyful and moved by pity (Psa. 78:40; Deut. 1:37; 1 Kings 3:10; Zeph. 3:17; Judg. 2:18). Expressing profound joy, God even sings with delight over His children (Zeph. 3:17).

We are made in the image of God and so we too are right to be angry about injustice. We can be angry without sinning. In the midst of anger, there can be a lot of shouting and finger pointing. Claiming high moral ground and calling for social justice for all, sweeping statements are often made and stereotypes reinforced. Some years ago, Janet Street-Porter, journalist and broadcaster, said that we had become a 'shouty society'.[2] She lamented that we have lost our ability to disagree agreeably, dialogue sensibly or listen with a willingness to change the cherished opinions that we clutch so tightly in a vice-like grip of our own sense of rightness. Sadly, I can see her point of view. We'll never move forward if we just lob verbal grenades at others, retreat and then huddle together for cover with those who are surely right because they agree with us. There is another side-effect to all the shouting: by focusing on the failures and foibles of others, it reduces our ability to see the flaws and faults in ourselves. To use the metaphor that Jesus chose, we go hunting for specks in other people's eyes, while being ignorant of, or blatantly ignoring, the huge planks in our own.

This book is a collection of stories designed to challenge, inspire, express vulnerability, show more kindness and be less swift to judge. And, yes, I'd like us to laugh together a little as well. I'll introduce you to Nurse Gemma; tell you about a stranger who lit up an airport; and even share how I'm a little like an antique clock – and not just because of my vintage. It will get personal as I open up a box of love letters. There will be some tears, perhaps, when I tell about the day that an entire street of houses disappeared along with a precious friendship. You'll meet a couple who lost their child for three days. You'll hear about an angry evangelist who tragically lost his faith. And I'll introduce you to a young soldier who made a life and death decision during World War Two – a choice that profoundly affected yours truly.

I hope that you'll enjoy what follows. If you do, let me know, and if you don't, let me know – but please don't shout.

Jeff Lucas

01
Specks and planks

Settling down for breakfast in a rather posh restaurant, we soaked up the ambience of the place. There was a gorgeous old fireplace with logs smouldering, emitting that glorious smell of charred wood. The walls were bedecked with silk wallpaper, and waiters wearing waistcoats dashed here and there with platefuls of steaming food. Lovely.

Gentle background music, canned but well chosen, complemented the sedate atmosphere. But then suddenly everything changed. The music shifted into a twinkly rendition of *Baa Baa Black Sheep*, which played from beginning to end in about 20 seconds – and then repeated. And repeated again. And, incredibly, again. Ten minutes later, having heard the question to the aforementioned black sheep whether or not it had any wool, and discovering once again that indeed wool was plenteous – three bags full, in fact – we felt restless, agitated. Surely the CD or MP3 player had got stuck. Other diners were frowning, following the great British tradition of noticing that something was wrong, not actually saying anything about it so as not to cause a fuss but looking forward to the opportunity of grumbling later.

Ten minutes later the sheepish repetition was beginning to feel like a musical version of some form of water torture, and so I decided to raise the issue with a passing waiter. 'Excuse me, can I just ask, what's going on with the music?' He tilted his head to one side, adopting the posture of one who wants to communicate that they are listening intently, and agreed: 'Yes sir, that *is* odd. I'll check.' Off he went and restarted the player, only now there were two tracks playing simultaneously, a cacophonic collision between Bach and those irritating sheep.

Other diners, emboldened by my enquiry to the waiter, moved into stage one of British complaining, which involves rolling one's eyes and sighing. (The next stage would be full-on huffing and puffing, but we were not quite there yet.) The waiter returned to our table, looking bewildered. It was then that the awful, hideous moment came, and the memory of it makes me cringe even as I record it here. The waiter pointed to a handbag owned by one of our group. 'The music is coming from that bag... your bag!' he cried triumphantly with a glee normally associated with a detective who has cracked a difficult whodunnit case. And indeed the music *was* emanating from that bag. Somehow a mobile phone had clicked on to a kids' app, which was playing *Baa Baa Black Sheep* over and over and over again. Suddenly the eye-rolling and sighing around the restaurant was replaced by chilly glares in our direction. I felt the frost. I had complained but *we* were the source of the irritation. Frustrated by the repetition, we were blissfully unaware that we were the ones to blame. Guilty as charged, m'lud.

In Matthew's Gospel, Jesus tells a story reminiscent of Monty Python. A hapless chap runs around with a magnifying glass, mustard keen to identify specks of sawdust in the eyes of others, but all along oblivious to the whacking great plank that sticks out from his own head (Matt. 7:1–5). Apparently, this 'plank' in Jesus' day would have been the main support for a house, which would have made it about 12 metres long – a significant protrusion. Sadly, this farcical scene is frequently played out, especially in churches. Fault-finding souls, eager to catch people doing or believing something that is suspect, patrol around searching for someone or something to correct. Sometimes they get together to form squadrons. When they find something that appears to be amiss, they pounce on it with unseemly joy, thrilled by yet another opportunity to highlight a problem or see others fail.

There is a German word for perverse delight, *schadenfreude*, which literally means 'harm joy' – the peculiar pleasure people derive from others' misfortune. Sometimes we're secretly thrilled when others stumble because we've simmered with envy at their success. Or we justify being glad at their stumbling by claiming a sense of justice – it's only right that they were exposed, they got what they deserved. Some psychologists believe that we are more likely to pop open a cork in celebration over the failure of others when we dehumanise them: viewing them as objects of scrutiny rather than real, flesh and blood human beings much loved by God. We take a pathological view, seeing them as exhibits rather than people. Ironically, when we do this, our unkind, cruel attitude might be far worse than the issue that we are determined to correct, but we can remain blissfully unaware of this. Perhaps we take up fault-finding as a hobby to spare ourselves the demanding discomfort of self-discovery. Peering at others through a magnifying glass is so much easier than staring at ourselves in a mirror. If we're in the habit of locating sawdust specks, perhaps it's time to focus more on what we're often blind to – our own faults and foibles.

Meanwhile, back at breakfast, the sheepish serenade was hastily silenced and calm was restored, but I still felt the need to depart in haste because the glares continued. Nobody likes a picky complainer. 'I think a rather huge apology to the staff is required,' boomed a chap at the next table, and I complied, begging forgiveness from the grinning waiters.

Who knows? If you have been a plank-sprouting-speck-hunting picky person, it might be that you are the cause of some grief. Perhaps in your life, a rather huge apology is required somewhere too.

02
Following

I've written about it extensively because the occasion was very significant for me, both in terms of commitment and embarrassment: my baptism. I decided to sing (and when I sing, people cry out to God in prayer that I might stop). The song, which I composed especially for the occasion, was cheesy and lengthy. If you're interested in hearing the six-verse epic, you can order the album I recorded, *Songs the Lord rejected* (£14.99, published by Music to Go Mad By). Not only that, but when I went under the water, I kicked my legs up, drenching some perfectly innocent members of the congregation who were sitting on the front row.

However, two elements of the evening linger in my memory for more positive reasons. Before each person stepped down into the tank of tepid water to be baptised, they were given a verse from the Bible to mark the occasion. My verse was Jeremiah 33:3: 'Call to me and I will answer you and tell you great and unsearchable things you do not know.' This was comforting because, although I had received a clear call to Christian leadership shortly after giving my life to Christ,

I was totally ignorant of all things biblical. Just four years after my baptism, my wife, Kay, and I were leading a church plant. I was 21 years old and Kay was 18. We were blessed with a patient and long-suffering congregation that smiled encouragingly while being told how to live by a couple barely out of adolescence. But we were also sustained by the knowledge that God would fill in the blanks for us and teach us as we journeyed.

Back at the baptism, there was one other aspect of the evening that stands out. As I emerged dripping (and, in my case, with the front row also dripping), the whole congregation sang the chorus of Robert Lowry's famous hymn:

Follow, follow, I would follow Jesus,
Anywhere, everywhere, I would follow on;
Follow, follow, I would follow Jesus,
Everywhere He leads me, I would follow on.

As a fresh-faced young lad, I sang that hymn without reservation or too much thought. My life was simple. At that point, I was single without responsibilities, without a mortgage and without a family to provide for. Time has passed and the 17-year-old with lots of hair has morphed into a 64-year-old with less hair. The long locks, once permed (what was I thinking?) have been replaced by a shrinking peninsula that used to looked like Texas on the top of my head but now has receded into something reminiscent of the Isle of Wight. But there have been other, more substantial changes.

The new believer that was me was handed a set of biblical

beliefs, which I accepted without question. After all, what did I know? Four decades on, the foundations still remain sure. As for some of the details, I now have a theological 'pending' file where I place subjects about which I have become less certain.

There have been some battles along the way. I've seen the best and worst of the Church. I've sat at boardroom tables of Christian organisations and have witnessed some appalling behaviour. I know what it feels like to enable a platform of opportunity for others only to be let down and betrayed. I've watched as respected fellow leaders have misappropriated funds, had inappropriate relationships or become ensnared by addiction. None of this is mentioned to elicit sympathy for myself, I just want to be honest about the trek so far.

However, there is one person who has disappointed me the most. Me. I rather expected that by now I would be better at praying, holier, more patient… the list could go on. I rather thought that I would be a little more grown up than I am at this stage of life. But this much is sure: Jesus has been unendingly kind to me. Most of the time, I don't know what He is doing; some of the time, I don't like what I think He's doing. But this I do know: He is good, beautiful, gracious and generous. So, I still want to follow Him, and I hope it's true that I'd be willing to do that anywhere, everywhere as that old song says. Surely being 'all grown up' is not about arrival, it's about daily continuing the journey. I don't feel 100% mature in my ministry, but I am still pursuing maturity.

Permit me one more song, again on that theme of following. It's a song that was popular at the huge evangelistic events led by the late, great Billy Graham:

I have decided to follow Jesus;
I have decided to follow Jesus;
I have decided to follow Jesus;
No turning back, no turning back.

It's said that the song is based on the last words of an Indian martyr, Nokseng, who converted to Christianity in the middle of the nineteenth century. A group of Welsh missionaries came into his community, spreading the message of love, peace and hope of Jesus Christ but received a hostile reception. Nokseng's family, however, came to Christ. Soon many other villagers began to accept Christianity, which incensed the village chief who called a public meeting and challenged the believers to renounce their faith in public or face execution. Moved by the Holy Spirit, Nokseng replied, 'I have decided to follow Jesus,' based on Luke 9:57. Even after his family were killed in front of him, he stood firm. Finally, Nokseng was also executed.

That husband and father stood firm under gargantuan pressure. The Bible encourages us to stand firm on the evil day, and what an evil day Nokseng experienced as he watched his family be executed and then went to his own death. To be honest, I find it hard to relate to such heroic faith. I'm rather certain that I'd respond differently if someone was pointing a gun or an arrow at my wife and children. But having decided to follow all those years ago, I don't want to turn back. I'd like to stand firm. I affirm my life choice anew.

Recommitment is good and there's precedent for it. Peter was invited by Jesus to follow Him. Three years later, Peter was given the opportunity to affirm his love and loyalty to Christ once again. Peter had seen the best and worst of himself. Stunned by his own betrayal, red-faced over his sword-swinging that could have cost a chap one of his ears, and counted among those who fled when Jesus was arrested, Peter was now given the chance to reaffirm his decision to follow. That recommitment included a newsflash from Jesus: an ongoing choice to follow Him would ultimately lead to Peter's arrest and death. He would live the rest of his life on a prophetic death row. But, undeterred, sobered by the sacrifice, thrilled by the vision, he made his choice, and in choosing became a world changer.

Today, whatever is past, whatever is now and whatever is ahead, may this description be true of us: we love Jesus, and follow Him, all the way home.

03

Forever-fascinating Father

The little girl shifted uncomfortably in the unyielding church pew, squirming for the twentieth time in two minutes. The plastic toy brought along to entertain her, an object of fascination and delight for the first half hour, was discarded now. The service had been so utterly dull. The sermon was about eternity – the preacher apparently illustrating this by speaking for what felt like forever – and the little girl was becoming desperate. After a wonderful moment of hope where it looked like a blissful conclusion was imminent, the preacher droned on and there were still two hymns and an offering to come. 'Mummy,' she hissed, a little too loudly, while pointing at the preacher, 'If we give him the money now, do you think he'll let us go?' That child has my sympathy. I've sat through quite a few mind-numbing Christian events myself, trying to look interested, while privately fantasising about forming an escape committee.

The Christian Church has had its fair share of horrible history and grave sins. One doesn't need to search too deeply to uncover the stains and scandals of the Church's past, our past. The Crusaders not only massacred Jews and Muslims but felt that heaven heartily cheered with each bloody swing of the sword. Catholics and Protestants took it in turns in their heresy hunts, burning each other alive, apparently oblivious to the irony that their fight was often over the nature of bread and wine – a symbolic act where Christians lovingly share communion together. Not much love there. There were popes unashamed and unblushing in their debauchery, the Salem witch trials, abuses of innocents by the clergy… the list could go on and on. Our history is sullied.

Then there are more subtle sins of the Church. Mindless legalism that has choked the life out of faith as believers sweated to please an unsmiling deity who could never be satisfied no matter how much they tried. There have been countless ugly dissensions and church splits when the family of God have fussed and fought, often over trivia like moving the pulpit, replacing the organ, painting the church kitchen, or, heaven help us, ditching the pews. Our sins are many. But there's something else I'd like to add to the list, and I think it's rather serious. It's the transgression of making the God of the universe appear boring. Too often the world has seen a ponderous, dull church and decided that the deity must be dull too. It's hardly surprising that a tedious god has been dismissed by so many with an indifferent yawn.

God is absolutely fascinating and endlessly intriguing. His creative brushstrokes come from a palette of billions of colours and shades. An unusual combination of engineer and artist, He sculpts and shapes the beautiful and bizarre, conjuring up no less than 300,000 species of beetles and weevils. He is the great poet, offering His struggling followers that epic blockbuster, the book of Revelation. The great dramatist, He grabs the attention of His wayward people with the real-life story of a prophet commanded to marry a whore. Dependable He is. Dull He most certainly is not.

Then along comes us Christians. Somehow, we've successfully wrapped this most spectacular personality into a vanilla, musty shroud of predictability and even tedium. Evidence of our remarkable gift in making God seem bland and uninteresting is everywhere; for example, in that funny and relatable sketch where Mr Bean battles sleep as the minister blathers on. By contrast, an exuberant black American bishop breaks through the crust of pomp and tradition at a royal wedding, communicating with zest, wit and charm, and the nation is intrigued, surprised to observe such vitality in the Church. It's not that there aren't vibrant churches; but what's undeniable is that we church folk have a reputation for sleepy solemnity. That's not to suggest that church services always have to be exciting with everyone on the edge of ecstasy. Churches that insist that everyone be always thrilled with life may struggle when suffering makes an unwelcome call. But surely we can be authentic, relevant, creative and biblical. Perhaps Christians can seem boring because we're just a little bored, especially if we've been believers for a while. Our faith is a yawn of familiarity because the good news is still good, but just not *news*. It's been said that 'Christian truths are unknown – because they're so well known.'

John, a member of Jesus' original team, knew more about Jesus at that point in history than anyone else on earth. One of the first to be chosen, he penned the fourth Gospel and had a front-row seat view of many miracles. The only one of the Twelve at the cross and trusted with the care of Jesus' mother, John saw Jesus in His transfiguration, crucifixion, resurrection and ascension. But there is still more to know about God, much more, as the last book of the Bible so powerfully demonstrates.

So let's ask this enthralling God to grant us a fresh glimpse of who He is, realising that in the here and now, our understanding of Him is but a teaspoon of water out of the vastness of the Pacific Ocean. Getting to grips with His love, which is so deep, so wide and so strong, would take forever but it's going to be a very, very interesting forever, because He is so absolutely fascinating.

04

 Divine applause

Doris, a thin, elderly lady, had been rushed to Accident and Emergency in the middle of the night. The duty doctor, knowing that the end was very near, wanted to spare Doris the indignity of dying on a hospital trolley. He wanted her to breathe her last in the warm comfort of a bed with her family gathered around her. Sadly, death was stalking Doris. Her breathing had become irregular and her vital organs were showing signs of closing down. 'At the most,' the doctor said to nurse Gemma, 'she has 20 minutes. Make her comfortable.'

The porter wheeled Doris into a side room, her distraught family members following on. Gemma and the porter carefully lifted Doris into the bed. Gemma placed a pillow beneath her head and spoke gently to the tearful family. 'Hold her hand. Whisper quietly if you like. It won't be long now.' Gemma then stepped out of the room to allow them some privacy. That's when everything took a strange turn. Just outside the room, another nurse arrived and began a conversation with Gemma that became more and more animated. She told Gemma how she had got hopelessly lost driving to a job interview at another hospital that day. Looking for the hospital, she had ended up in a local park and somehow managed to drive her car right onto a bowling green – in the middle of a game! The more the story unfolded, the more Gemma laughed. What began as a stifled giggle turned into a deep, raucous belly laugh. Not one normally given to laughing out loud, Gemma howled for quite some minutes, the sound echoing down the dark corridor. But then she realised that, behind the thin plasterboard wall, just a few feet away, a lady was dying, relatives were weeping and her laughter was quite out of place. She dried her eyes and steeled herself to apologise to the family for her inappropriate behaviour.

Opening the door, she saw Doris sitting up in bed. Doris had removed her oxygen mask and was now giggling at her stunned relatives.

'Are you alright?' asked Gemma, amazed.

'Well, dear,' said Doris, her eyes sparkling, 'I heard this sound of beautiful laughter, and I wanted to join in. The laughter was so lovely, so I laughed along, woke up, and here I am. Are you the one with the lovely laugh?'

The delightful conversation that followed revealed that both Gemma and Doris were Christians. Gemma didn't lose her job, and Doris didn't lose her life. The next day the doctors pronounced her perfectly fit enough to go home. She had laughed her way back into life. All of that happened 13 years ago. I have shared that story around the world in preaching and in print, and I thought that was the end of it. But there is a postscript.

Four decades ago, I was at Bible college with Graham and Linda, Gemma's parents. The last time I heard from them or Gemma directly was over a decade ago, but just recently, Linda posted a one-line encouraging comment on my Facebook page. It prompted me to ask how their daughter was doing during these days of coronavirus-induced challenge. I also felt nudged to make contact with Gemma directly to let her know I was praying for her. The thought persisted, but I got distracted and didn't do it. (I tend to be spiritually slow.) Then, a few days later, an email arrived from Colorado. A woman had heard the Doris and Gemma story and so identified with it that she had named her daughter Gemma. She wanted to know if she could include the story in a baby book. What are the chances of these two events happening so close together after 13 long years?

I called Gemma who was now responsible for training fellow nurses to deal with patients with COVID-19. The scenes at her hospital were harrowing, and she had been asking God: *How will I be remembered? Am I making a difference in the world?* How thrilled and encouraged she was to hear of a baby in America named Gemma!

There was a final joy. Connecting with Gemma's parents, I discovered that they had both been ill with the COVID-19 virus. Thankfully, Linda was recently discharged from hospital, having narrowly escaped death. Graham had also recovered. Understandably, they have been anxious for Gemma's health and wellbeing, working on the front line. They too were so encouraged about the baby named after their daughter.

What a privilege it was to stand on our doorsteps, bang drums, blow whistles and clap for our NHS heroes and all those involved in social care. But the events surrounding the birth of a baby named Gemma suggests to me that, when we were cheering them on, perhaps accompanied by saucepan bashing angels, God was joining in with the applause.

05
Palm Sunday in lockdown

A major symptom of lockdown is lethargy. That's right, and I'd like to talk about it… if I can be bothered. Lethargy (which is not the word 'liturgy' spoken with a lisp) is a symptom that I believe affects many of us.

It's Palm Sunday as I write, the day when, figuratively speaking, we should all be scaling up palm trees (don't do it in shorts), and cutting down palm fronds, so that we can wave them as our Messiah rides by on a donkey. It's the day when the cry of 'Hosanna!' should be in our throats. The hope of the world is riding into town. The cavalry has arrived to save us. Hip hip hooray!

But here's the thing. There's no crowds this year: they're all thinned out by social distancing, and rightly so. We might find ourselves wanting to observe Holy Week, but feeling tired, flat and weary – and somewhat unholy as a result.

'Where doth this lethargy cometh from?' I hear you ask (those of you who have been reading the King James version of the Bible because you've got time on your hands). Well, for one thing, we're inactive. Yes, we can go out for exercise, but the sight of an approaching stranger nudges us into multi-layered apprehension. What if they are carriers of the dreaded pox? And then, what side of the path or pavement should I occupy? Do normal highway code rules apply (keep to the left when in the UK)? Why aren't they moving over to play their part in the distancing routine? And then, as we pass, should we greet them even briefly, expelling something called 'droplets' in the process? Should we smile, wish them well, or just scurry on? Is the masked person someone taking extra distancing precautions, or are they in fact a bank robber on their way home from a failed job (they went to rob the bank, but like everything else, it was closed)? We're not sure whether we should smile and nod – or call the police.

We watch TV and are overwhelmed by a continual flow of bad news, daunting statistics and speculation. In order to get away from real-life drama, hypocrisy, political bluster and death, we binge-watch Netflix or BBC iPlayer, which provide endless episodes of fictional drama, hypocrisy, political bluster and death.

We are grateful for national leaders who we hope are doing their best and heartened by health-worker heroes who are risking their own health for us. We hear talk of the front line, appropriately drawing on wartime language. The self-sacrificial giving of others creates a sense of powerlessness in us. What, if anything, can *we* do to help? We're told that our greatest contribution is to stay at home and save lives – true but it seems like a paltry effort.

In lockdown, there's less 'So, what did you do today?' chatter, because we all know what we did – stayed at home. Hearing the headlines, we rehearse them to each other. On top of that, we feel for those who have to steer through lockdown alone.

All in all, some of us feel various degrees of emotional flatness. And that's perfectly understandable. We should grieve when young nurses die. We should care about what will happen to the disadvantaged around the world. We should recognise that we were created for productivity, and when our capacity to deliver, produce, complete and resolve is limited, we feel stunted. We are suffering the effects of a seismic shock, thrust suddenly into a Bruce Willis disaster movie, one in which Brucie has yet to rescue us from the approaching meteor or, in this case, the lurking virus. Being around friends and family is precious, so it's understandable that we feel a sense of lack, even impoverishment, when we cannot connect, laugh, dine with and hug those we love.

On Palm Sunday, we who follow Christ still reach for a palm branch. Our arms might be tired as we wave it, and our cry of 'Hosanna' might feel just a little hollow. We feel a little silly, waving bits of a tree without a crowd or a physical congregation to bolster our hearts. Praying can feel dutiful, and while there have been rays of light and heartening stories, significant divine infiltration is yet to be forthcoming. It's not easy, but our emotions are not the barometer of our spirituality. Just because we are disheartened does not mean our faith is lacking. Let's look past the headlines to the one who has ridden through the city, died, rose again and will return one day. Let's trust Him even when we don't know for certain what He is doing. His hand is not always easy to trace. When we do not see the obvious move of His hand, we trust His heart and know that it is moved. When we feel nudged towards hopelessness, faith affirms that He is still our hope. When we follow the cross, we follow in the steps of our Christian ancestors, some of whom walked to martyrdom and trusted God till their final breath.

So, go ahead, pick up that palm branch, weary soul. Give it a wave. You know it makes sense.

06
Prayer during lockdown

During lockdown, I found it quite difficult to pray. Actually, I find it challenging to pray at the best of times. It didn't take a global pandemic to challenge my intercessory ability. Chatting with someone who is invisible is not something that comes easy to me. Some people describe prayer as a conversation. Sadly, it isn't for me. There are times – all too rare – where I have a sense that God is directly communicating to me, but mostly I feel as though I am twiddling the knob of an old transistor radio. I get a sudden splurge of voice, quickly obliterated by static. When I try to retune, it turns out I was picking up Russian Folk Music FM.

I had rather expected that a world crisis would focus and even embolden my praying. This is because I am rather good at screaming when under pressure, so I anticipated the same fervency, clarity and intensity in prayer when under pressure shared by the rest of the planet. Unfortunately, that has not been the case.

I'm not sure I can describe it adequately but the crisis has changed me, and now – off the wall as it sounds – I feel that I need to reintroduce myself to Jesus. Of course, that's not necessary because I believe that I am utterly known by Him, but there's been such a shift in my priorities, such turbulence in my moods, and, along with everyone else, such a change in my everyday lifestyle that I feel unfamiliar with myself. I feel that I need to update Jesus on the adjustments, and perhaps get some insight about the alterations to myself. But where do I begin?

There's so much to pray about, so many needs, problems, challenges, statistics, predictions, hopes, fears… they overwhelm like a tsunami. Where to begin? Having too much to pray for is just as challenging as not knowing what to say. That's why liturgy can be helpful – especially when life renders us speechless. It's rather wonderful to use the well-crafted words shaped by someone who lived a few hundred years ago.

Then there's the challenge of praying about some of the problems in my life – I have discovered that they were small. I wish that I could go back to worrying about what made me anxious before the pandemic took hold. The trouble is, for the most part, I can't remember what I was worrying about.

Any difficulties I've faced have all been relative to the greater problem of COVID-19.

There have been a couple of examples of God activity in my own personal life. (I'd like to call them answers to prayer but I hadn't asked for them to happen, so I can't claim them as an answer – drat.) But although I find some strength and hope in these minor interventions, I am mostly embarrassed by them. They seem rather trivial, silly even. I'm tempted to send an email to gabriel@heavensgates.com. It would go something like:

Dear Gabe (if I may be so bold; 'Gabe' feels a bit familiar as most humans who meet you almost faint in shock, so I hope this is okay),

I write to thank you, your angelic pals and, most of all, the Lord of heaven and earth for all of your snippets of involvement in my life. Although we've never met face to face (and I'm not requesting an imminent appointment, especially if it involves a pearly-gate encounter and thus my death), I have, over the years, been extremely grateful for all the positive interventions from heaven in my minuscule little life here on earth.

I am going to regret writing this as soon as I send it, desperate as I am for the continuation of the aforementioned (and did I say most welcome?) activities in the journey of yours truly.

Nevertheless, perhaps you could pass this message on to our heavenly Father. I would like to ask Him one small request: that He moves to save the inhabitants of planet Earth from this virus thingy. I call it a thingy because, as I write, even the most eminent scientists in the world, in their collective collaborating of their huge brains, have not been able to figure it out. Calling it by name, COVID-19, does make us feel a little better, as if it's something we identify, dissect and then destroy. For many years now, I and my fellow human beings have lived under the collective illusion that we are rather clever and can control our own destinies. We were lulled into this silly myth as a result of:

(a) not having a world war for a while;

(b) only engaging in localised wars, which were mostly far away, so we chose to ignore them;

(c) ignoring mass poverty and environmental destruction, for reasons unknown.

Recent developments have proved that we are not actually masters of the universe – that position being filled by your Lord and mine.

Anyway, back to the reason for my emailing you. I wonder if you could let it be known that you and the rest of heaven's vast army can forget about my little worries and just sort out this horrid virus. (Hold on… Let me delete that last sentence, or at least amend it.) Please forget me suggesting that you forget my little worries, just *postpone* giving them your attention because I'd rather like you to return to giving your attention to my stuff once this pandemic is over with.

In the meantime, I hope it will be alright to offer this short prayer to the Lord – a piece of simple liturgy, if you will: Lord God, Help! Help! Help! Amen.

Yours sincerely,
Jeff

PS Please don't forget that I changed 'forget' into 'postpone'. Thanks.

07
Weathering the storm clouds

Reduced to tears by the televised heartfelt tributes to loved ones who have died because of COVID-19, I felt heavy. I know it's OK to feel that way, but perhaps I need to take a step further and say that it's human and needful to feel low at times. That which usually makes my heart sing was taken away during lockdown: the hugs of grandsons, the fun of a meal shared with family and friends, the physical gathering of fellow believers for worship, the simple joy of popping into town for a coffee. I find so much joy in those moments that when they are denied for a period of time, I tend to feel vacant and flat. Water slakes thirst. Lack of water makes your lips dry. Simple, unavoidable fact.

When I'm feeling low, I want to lecture myself sternly, to wave my own finger in front of my own face and tell the rather glum me that it's worse – so, so much worse – for others around the country and in the wider world. And that's very true. But the lecture doesn't quite work, because despite my relatively pain-free existence, there's still some sadness. That cloud is not driven away by me just comparing my weather conditions with someone else's storm. I need to stay aware of what's happening in the world, though, otherwise my capacity for self-absorption can grow out of control – like my hair has a habit of doing when I can't get to the hairdresser.

So, what to do when sorrow presses down? I'm trying to take baby steps. Aiming just to get the next thing done. Praying some one-sentence prayers. Being grateful for small things. Reading something fun, then something deeper and then something biblical (and not necessarily in that order). And I'm learning how to rejoice. Most of the encouragements towards rejoicing in the Bible were written to or by people that were experiencing extremely tough times, like Paul who experienced such pressure and pain.

We will get through the storm. Right. Baby steps.

08
Cause and effect

Our secret hoard is safely secreted behind lock and key, housed in a plain-looking cardboard box, away from prying eyes. I hope it will never be discovered, except after Kay and I have passed away and are beyond the excruciating embarrassment we'd feel if the contents of our awful stash were revealed.

That box contains a stack of love letters that we exchanged when we first met. A couple of bright young Christian things, relatively new in the faith, we were *very* enthusiastic about Jesus. I wore my passion for Him on my sleeve or, more specifically, on my lapel, wearing badges like 'Don't get caught dead without Jesus', which was only slightly better than 'Eternity – smoking or non-smoking?'. Another classic was, 'My boss is a Jewish carpenter', which, on reflection, is a rather inadequate description of the risen, ascended, glorified Christ. My evangelistic lapel was also occasionally dotted with silvery doves and fishes. Some surely wondered if I was a pigeon fancier or a member of the International Association of Cod Fryers.

We were genuinely keen to put God first in our lives, as evidenced in those letters. A mixture of religious fervency and heady romantic slush, they are exhibits that prove that we were falling deeply but nervously in love, seeing as we were rather neurotic about the possibility of loving anything or anybody more than Jesus. The letters say it all – literally. I dazzled my then-girlfriend with such epithets as 'Dear Sister Kay, I think you're gorgeous. Hallelujah!' but then quickly affirmed my determined discipleship with 'I love you so much but I love Jesus more. Praise the Lord. Glory to God.'

OK, I didn't actually address her as *Sister* Kay – that would have been a bridge way too far, and I'd have felt like I was dating a nun, but the rest is for real. Yikes. I flush crimson as I recall them. Our hearts were in the right place, but our words were cheesy beyond belief. However, the core message of these nauseous little epistles, apart from the religious intensity, was this: *because* I love you, *therefore* I will do anything for you. A cause created an effect. Through His Word, God speaks to us in rather the same way, and always has.

The Ten Commandments were given after God rescued those hapless Hebrews from their Egyptian oppressors. It has been said that those commands were not only written in stone but in story. God's call to a kingdom lifestyle came after He had demonstrated His loving care. *Because* I've rescued you, *therefore* live like this.

The *because* and *therefore* of love are found in the New Testament too, most strongly in Paul's words to his friends in Rome: '*Therefore*, I urge you, brothers and sisters, *in view of God's mercy,* to offer your bodies as a living sacrifice, holy and pleasing to God – this is your true and proper worship (Rom. 12:1, emphasis added). We obey not that God might love us but because we are already greatly loved and have found grace and mercy.

There's been a lot of furore in America over the removal of the Ten Commandments from courthouses and other public buildings. The Commandments are listed but often without the reason behind them; legislation lifted out of the context of story. No hint of *because* and *therefore*. Divorced from a relationship with God, they sound like clinical, cold prohibitions from a cosmic killjoy. Surely the Ten Commandments, while also being the basis of healthy living and relationships, are primarily covenant words for covenant people. The brilliant Stanley Hauerwas is candid:

> The commandments are not guidelines for humanity in general. They are a countercultural way of life for those who know who they are and whose they are. Their function is not to keep… culture running smoothly, but rather to produce a people who are, in our daily lives, a sign, a signal, a witness that God has not left the world to its own devices.[1]

Too often, we, the Church, have been guilty of ranting, insisting that our culture get in step with God's ways, instead of humbly demonstrating His heart in our everyday walk with Him. May we have a greater grasp of the truth that is so basic and fundamental, yet one that we'll likely spend an eternity beginning to understand: we are beloved of God.

That being true, we respond with love and commitment. Because… and therefore.

By the way, amazingly, those soppy letters worked. Forty-four years on, Kay and I continue our journey together.

Hallelujah. Praise the Lord.

09

Looking back, moving forward

He or she who endeavours to teach their offspring to drive, truly it shall be a curse unto them. Ride not in thine child's chariot, and longer (and calmer) shall thy life be upon the earth. So says the wise man in the book of Proverbs. Or maybe it is Ecclesiastes.

Please step away from the concordance, and don't email me to complain, because, obviously, no such verse occurs anywhere in the Bible. That's unfortunate because a prohibition about parents teaching their adult children to drive would have been helpful. I'm embarrassed to report my lack of patience – and occasional high-pitched screaming – when I tried to play driving instructor as well as dad. Those of us who are parents will know that we tend to remember our worst moments in raising our children, and when I think of my own shortcomings, my attempts at being a driving instructor come quickly to mind and cause a blush of shame. But I also remember a mantra often repeated during those tense, nail-biting lessons. Mirror, signal, manoeuvre. Mirror, signal, manoeuvre. In other words, be sure that you look behind you before you change lane or direction. That way, you'll avoid having a metallic encounter with something rather solid, like a juggernaut.

Mirror, signal, manoeuvre. Wise advice indeed, not only for driving but for life itself. Paraphrasing Søren Kierkegaard's famous quote: *Life is lived forwards, but is understood backwards.* Our eyesight tends to be keener when we carefully look back.

I originally wrote these thoughts after having emerged from that festival of forward thinking: New Year's Eve. Wearied by bruising Brexit rhetoric, see-sawing financial markets and weather only exciting to Eskimos, we gladly waved goodbye to 2019. Teetering on the brink of the then-unsullied 2020, we peered hopefully ahead. Resolutions were made and goals for the coming year were set. We raised a glass and chinked a toast, keen for better days ahead. We had no idea then that something called coronavirus was waiting in the wings, poised to make such a tragic entrance.

Looking positively ahead is healthy but looking back is vital too. Some Christians are always hunting for a fresh word from God, a revelation, but neglect the treasure that might be buried in their past, wisdom. We don't have to look far in Scripture to see wisdom celebrated. 'The beginning of wisdom is this: get wisdom. Though it cost all you have, get understanding' (Prov. 4:7). (It really says that. I didn't make that one up!)

Called to march forward into the Promised Land, the

people of Israel were commanded to regularly look back. Failure to do so led to their wilderness meanderings. God's people tasted their past as they ate unleavened bread, celebrating the Passover. Their story was scribbled on their doorposts. People wore their story, tying symbols on their hands and forehead. What had been before was recalled by altars and stone pillars, marking the spots of historic triumphs or theophanies (encounters with God).

When building the Temple, furniture makers carved their past story in wood, sculptors sculpted it, metalworkers hammered it and jewellers set the story in precious stones. The story was smelled as incense was offered. It was acted out through the elaborate sacrificial system. It was even chimed as the priestly bells sounded. The festivals and gatherings were regular opportunities for covenant renewal, evaluation and definition, enabling the people of God to question themselves: *Have we been faithful to the covenant? Where have we failed?* Retrospection led to repentance. Things went badly wrong when they forget who they were and where they'd come from.

So perhaps we would do well to look back, and not just when 31 December comes around again. This is more than nostalgia. Rose-tinted spectacles must be removed. There will be moments of gratitude as we trace the finger of God; faith will be nurtured as we celebrate the truth that the one who has helped us will help us still. Perhaps there will be some regret when we see the tracks of our own wanderings. Undoubtably there will be some vital lessons reinforced as we recall them and determine not to repeat our follies. Most of all, considering our yesterdays will help us navigate healthily into our tomorrows.

Mirror, signal, manoeuvre.

10

 Phone a friend

Bognor Regis. I know. Despite its regal title, it's never going to make the 'Top Exotic Locations in the World' list. Any readers who are residents or who love the place look away now (or forgive me) because here's the truth: glorious white sand is in rather short supply; the beach is a mass of unyielding pebbles, making barefoot bathers wince as they pick their way across to the water's edge. There's a broken pier, shattered by a series of devastating storms and fires. Once the home of a fabulous 1,400-seat theatre, the pier is now a sad, short iron stump jutting out into the grey sea with only a tired amusement arcade flashing neon lights intermittently. There's a smell of damp and seaweed heavy in the air… but Bognor holds a special place in my heart.

It was in Bognor Regis that my brand-new bride and I went to church, the Sunday morning after our Saturday wedding. Discovering that we were newlyweds, the minister asked me to give a word of testimony about my most recent blessings. This being the morning after our wedding night, I blushed crimson red. Awkward.

As a young lad, I spent some marvellous summers messing around on Bognor's beach. My grandparents lived just a few miles from the coast, and I would regularly stay with them in the summer holidays. I would board the bus near my grandparent's house (those were days when a 12-year-old was allowed to travel alone on a bus), and make my way to Bognor seafront to visit my friend Ian who lived very close to the promenade. I was always given a warm welcome by his family, even though I had not seen my friend for a whole year. We spent long, wonderful days, tanned deep brown by the salty sun. At the end of the afternoon, our tired limbs would be restored by delicious suppers served by Ian's mum. For a London boy, those days by the sea were heavenly. Until it happened.

It was the beginning of another long, lazy summer. Excited and eager to begin a few weeks of fun, I leapt off the bus and ran towards the street where Ian lived. I turned the corner, and my dream summer turned to winter in an instant. Ian's house had disappeared, vanished into thin air. Gone. How could this be? Who would steal a house?

Actually, the entire street had been swept away, all houses demolished, to make room for a new municipal car park. As for Ian and his family, I had no idea where they had gone, no way to make contact. That was that. I never saw him again.

Fifty years later, I still think about Ian and my soul sinks. I would love to know what happened to him; how his life turned out. How delightful it would be to meet up, to remember those carefree days that we shared. This led me to think about other friendships that I've enjoyed through the years, and to lament the fact that some friendships, which I thought would stay strong, are no more. Some close ties came undone due to conflict and misunderstanding. Other times, the flame of friendship faded because our bond couldn't stretch across the geographical distance between us. Or a role or function catalysed friendship, and when that season of working together ended, the friendships made in that shared space sadly ended too.

Sometimes there's a sudden ending. Jesus knew that pain of disappearing friendships. Mark's Gospel gives a stark indictment about His band of brothers: 'Then everyone deserted him and fled' (Mark 14:50). They vanished into thin air. Gone. I've had a few of those friendships. And I am sure that I have been a less-than-perfect friend. Sometimes when crises hit others, I was not there for them; other times I spoke words that I now regret and wish I could take back. As a friend, mine is a far from perfect record.

Friends make us better. We drink deep from joy's well when laughter is shared. A fabulous experience is so much better when we can turn to a friend and say, 'Isn't this great?' But this much is true: friends tell us what we don't know, and, if their friendship is deep, they'll tell us what we really don't *want* to know – when those planks appear in our eyes. Friends shape us even if they sometimes disappoint us because there's no perfect fit in friendship, and to think otherwise is naive. Friendship comforts, but also confronts our selfishness too. And friendship calls us to faithfulness, to hang in there and stick close – whether we feel like it or not. We need to love our friends for who they are, and not spend our days wishing that they'd be different.

So today, phone or email a friend, because a true friend is a treasure, and loneliness is literally punishing. Ironically, it took social distancing to teach us the value of togetherness.

And speaking of phone calls, there's one I'd especially welcome.

Ian, if, by some small chance, you're reading this, do me a huge favour, please give me a call.

11 People of the story

It all began when one of my grandsons asked me about our family history and I told him what I knew. As you'll read in more detail later in this book, my father, Stanley Lucas, was captured in North Africa in 1940. Held as a prisoner of war for four years in a camp just a few miles from Auschwitz, he finally escaped during a death march in what was the coldest winter in a hundred years. My grandfather, Walter Lucas, was awarded the Military Medal, honoured for the bravery he showed as a stretcher-bearer in the hellish trenches of the Great War. Anthony, my great-grandfather, was born in Cologne, Germany, and travelled to England, smuggled in a box. It's cost effective to travel in economy class, but I never quite understood why he chose that class of transport, until recently.

Signing up to an online genealogical search engine, I began to uncover further details, some of which are desperately sad. Anthony chose a box for travel because he was so gut-wrenchingly poor. Eventually he would be separated from his family and officially registered as a pauper, finding refuge in the gruelling conditions of an East London workhouse. The cause of his death was listed as shock. Both he and my great-grandmother ended their days apart in what were rather crudely dubbed as asylums. I learned about the awful conditions that they endured and wondered how they navigated every awful day.

Instead of a distant link to royalty, or perhaps a distinguished writer, what I uncovered was snapshots of ordinary people who fought to survive. I felt sad for them, grateful for the life I've lived, and a sense of location that I can't yet fully describe. My worries shrink into perspective, resized by their stories from yesteryear. The details of my family's heritage – some of it noble, some of it tragic – have laid dormant for too long, buried in record offices and scribbled on faded parchments. I am richer for my discoveries, and the quest for more insight continues. I have been nourished as I've uncovered the stories of those who have gone before.

We Christians are a storied people, but many of us don't really know that story. Too often the Bible stays unread, gathering dust on a shelf. We say that we believe that it is the Word of God to humanity, but the way we neglect it calls the integrity of that belief into question. Or we take a pick-and-mix approach to Scripture, not bothering to join the dots and see how it all links together so marvellously. In the Old Testament, the people of Israel were called to celebrate chapters in the story of God through feasts and festivals. They were commanded to remember the breathless epic of deliverance and exodus from Egypt and tell it to their children during the

Passover meal. Jesus called us believers to regularly huddle together to share bread and wine, not just as a community snack, but to help us to remember what really matters.

We can also help each other as we share our own personal stories of life and faith. The 'Testimony time' or 'Good news' slot used to be a regular feature in some church gatherings. Admittedly, some of the sharing was just a little awkward, as dear old Fred told us that Jesus had healed his hamster. We rejoiced that little Hammy was back in the wheel again, but underwhelmed with Fred's weekly health update. Perhaps we need to make space for more story-sharing in our church communities once more.

I regularly travel to the Holy Land with a group of pilgrims. We trek around the set of God's story, which comes alive once more as we look at ancient stones and holy sites. But each evening we gather to talk about some of our own backgrounds, experiences and learnings – living stones sharing together.

I'm glad I found out about my great-great-grandparent who served a prison sentence for poaching, which made that rabbit sandwich rather costly. But uncovering my family history caused me some anxiety. I carry their genes, so might I carry some of their negative traits. Thankfully, I was helped by words from Bishop Graham Tomlin in his excellent book *The Provocative Church*[1]:

...if you are a Christian, the story that tells you who you are is not the story of your parents, ancestors, ethnic group or social class. It is, instead, the story of the Bible – the *promise* to Abraham, *deliverance* from slavery to Egypt and sin, and the *gift* of land to landless Israelites and life to dead sinners. This story of promise, deliverance and gift is your family history, the story that defines you.

I'm glad to know where I come from, and I will continue the search to see if there are other insights from days gone by, but I'm also challenged to dig afresh into the big story in God's Word. I want to keep listening to the unfolding stories of God's people because, thanks to Jesus, I've not just been born, but born again, adopted into *His* family.

12
Lighting up the airport

Airports are not my favourite places, which is unfortunate because over the years I have spent quite a lot of time in them. I don't mind flying so much, even though some in-flight food is surely created by demonised chefs, and one is occasionally required to play that culinary game, 'Name that food', mainly because it is difficult to determine whether it is beef or chicken. Unlike the excited newbie traveller, the thrilled ten-year-old, or even that pencil-toting soul who goes plane-spotting (apologies to any pencil-toting plane-spotting souls who are reading this), I'm no longer joyous when I step inside a terminal. On the contrary.

Airports are usually emotional black holes. Admittedly, there are a few happy folk to be seen, although some of them have smiles fuelled by quaffing lager with their airport breakfast, a habit that is surely prohibited in Leviticus. Dark Irish stout is not the ideal beverage to go with eggs and bacon at 7am. Most people in airports are there simply because they want to be somewhere else, which affects their mood.

Then there's the security screening, where you try to look relaxed while your hand luggage is being scanned because there is the remote possibility that a tactical nuclear warhead has been secreted alongside your laptop. One of my most least favourite moments comes when I have to remove my belt. I have a deep-seated fear that one day my jeans will fall to my ankles and I will be hapless in a crowded security area, embarrassed beyond belief in my Mickey Mouse adorned boxer shorts. I could go on. There's all that rushing, because, sadly, some airport officials tell fibs. Actually, they lie. The departure board flashes up the news that your flight is now boarding, or even worse, is now in the final, 'last and final call' process. The gate is a 20-minute walk away, and so breathless and perhaps even muttering words not normally in the vocabulary of good Christian people, you arrive at the gate only to discover that the boarding process has not even started. You repent of muttering those words, but then you feel something close to hatred for the person who issued the false boarding announcement, and then you repent of feeling hatred...

Sorry, there's more! If you are flying a budget airline, you will be required to line up according to the seat number on your boarding pass. If you're in seat B23, may the Lord have mercy upon you if by accident you get in front of the person who is in seat B22. All in all, I'm usually glad when the time comes to exit the airport. I prefer arriving to travelling.

There was one particular occasion, however, when the sun came out in Denver airport terminal A, and all because of a lady that Kay and I had spotted. One of our hobbies is people watching – and people listening. Sometimes we take this a little too far, and refrain from conversation with each other so that we can tune in to the conversations of others nearby. (Kay especially loves this. With a birthday coming up, I'm planning on buying her surveillance equipment as a gift.)

As for the aforementioned lady, we first saw her on the swaying transit train that propelled us towards our gate area. Standing next to a nervous-looking family, she greeted them, all smiles, and wished them a happy flight. Just one warm comment from her seemed to calm their frayed nerves a little.

Later, when we boarded an escalator, she stood behind us and smiled and joked with a rather sullen-looking passenger too, brightening up the 20-second ascent. And then, to our surprise, she lined up for the same flight as us (bearing in mind that Denver airport normally has over 1,600 flights daily). As she boarded, she profusely thanked the gate agent, who seemed surprised and thrilled at the appreciation.

We took off, I popped a peanut in my mouth (unhelpfully adding to the dehydrating conditions of flying) and pondered her kindness. It was then that I felt a nudge, perhaps from God, to encourage her if I could find her once we'd landed. My mind immediately recoiled at the notion. The lady might not welcome an approach from a random chap. My well-meaning intentions could end up as an example in a 'Stranger Danger' public safety advice video.

After we'd landed and disembarked the plane, she was nowhere to be found. Frankly, I felt relieved; off the hook from what I'd thought might be a mission from God. Down in the busy baggage claim area, I dutifully scanned the crowd but in vain. And then I noticed that she was standing right next to me, talking on the phone. Suddenly her carry-on bag fell over at my feet. This could be my moment, but she was still talking as I put the bag upright. She thanked me mid-call, grabbed her bags, headed away and then stopped to look at her phone. Our luggage arrived, and we headed to walk past her – and that's when her bag fell over once more, again, right at my feet.

I plunged in nervously. 'Excuse me… this might sound a little strange, but I'm a pastor.' (I felt that might make me sound a little safer, which may or may not be the case.) 'My wife and I both noticed your repeated kindness back in Denver. It's so refreshing to see someone act like you do. I prayed that I would have the chance to meet you and thank you. And so… thank you!' Her mouth fell open, she smiled broadly – and then burst into tears. Happy tears.

After the briefest of chats, she hurried off to repair her ruined mascara. And I was left wondering: Had God performed some nifty choreography to enable that moment?

I'm wary of Christians who see God steering every detail of life. I no longer pray for parking spaces (unless I desperately need one), feeling that the Lord of the universe has other things to deal with. But my faith in coincidences is limited. We often say that the devil is in the detail, but perhaps, just perhaps, God is in the detail too. Did God set up that airport encounter? Possibly. Probably, even.

This much is absolutely certain: kindness, so wonderfully demonstrated by that smiling, gracious lady, can light up gloomier spaces. Kindness is an oft-overlooked characteristic of our God, who graced His old covenant people with loving-kindness. Paul, writing a letter to his friends in Ephesus, celebrated the God who 'has showered his kindness on us' (Eph. 1:8, NLT) in Christ Jesus. When we're kind, we're just a little more like God.

Kindness often costs nothing except time and thought, but surely turns heads and hearts here on earth. And surely heaven watches and celebrates acts of kindness as well.

13

 Losing Jesus

If Mary and Joseph were alive today, they would probably get a visit from a social worker.

I imagine the social worker as an intimidating female ambassador from social services, standing hands on hips on their humble threshold. Her blouse is severely buttoned right up to the neck, the downturned edges of her mouth a dour picture of disapproval.

'Sadly, we've received a disturbing report, which I am required to investigate,' she drones. Proffering an identity card, her voice is a flat monotone. 'Apparently, your 12-year-old son went missing while in your care.' She slows her speech and punctuates her words for effect. 'For Three. Whole. Days.'

There's more. 'Incredibly, we hear that you two didn't even notice your son was gone for a whole day. He was left alone in the city. May I come in?'

It's a well-known story from Luke's Gospel, found in Luke 2:41–52. Here it is in Eugene Peterson's, *The Message*:

Every year Jesus' parents traveled to Jerusalem for
the Feast of Passover. When he was twelve years old,
they went up as they always did for the Feast. When it
was over and they left for home, the child Jesus stayed
behind in Jerusalem, but his parents didn't know it.
Thinking he was somewhere in the company of pilgrims,
they journeyed for a whole day and then began looking
for him among relatives and neighbors. When they didn't
find him, they went back to Jerusalem looking for him.

The next day they found him in the Temple seated
among the teachers, listening to them and asking
questions. The teachers were all quite taken with him,
impressed with the sharpness of his answers. But his
parents were not impressed; they were upset and hurt.

His mother said, 'Young man, why have you done this
to us? Your father and I have been half out of our minds
looking for you.'

He said, 'Why were you looking for me? Didn't you
know that I had to be here, dealing with the things of my
Father?' But they had no idea what he was talking about.

So he went back to Nazareth with them, and lived
obediently with them. His mother held these things
dearly, deep within herself. And Jesus matured,
growing up in both body and spirit, blessed by both God
and people.

It's one of those curious Gospel stories that has always
troubled me. To my mind, Jesus' comment to His much-
relieved parents, 'Didn't you know that I had to be here,

dealing with the things of my Father?' sounds just a tad precocious. Don't write in; I'm not questioning His sinlessness, just confessing a worry.

Also let's think about how His mum and step-dad must have been feeling. When I'm on watch as a grandparent, I'm frantic if one of the lovely boys is out of my sight for more than a minute or two. Gone missing for three days? I'd be out of my mind. How on earth could they lose their son like that? OK, as a 12-year-old, He would be approaching His bar mitzvah, after which He'd be considered an adult. And it was common for communities to travel together, so perhaps Mary and Joseph just thought He was with Uncle Moshe. But still... Imagine their relief when at last they spotted Him, chatting with the religious barons in the Temple courts. There He is!

Switching the story around a little, perhaps losing Jesus is easy to do. Commenting on this episode in her beautifully frank book, *Still*[1], Lauren Winner makes a stark confession: 'I lose Jesus all the time.'

Me too. It's not that I lose Jesus in a once-and-for-all declaration of denial and unbelief, a solid act of rejection. I just mislay Him. I emerge from a heady spiritual mountaintop experience, perhaps after one of those conferences where wall-to-wall excitement is very much part of the programme. Religiously enthused, I quickstep down the road, assuming that because I met Him back there, that's He's alongside here. He'll catch up. Or I'm busy with the incidental, practising the laziness of frenetic activity, which means I neglect what's really important. Sometimes I stubbornly head away from Him; surely, I muse, He'll get in step with me –

at least eventually. Or instead of following Him (which is what everything is supposed to be about), I follow the ruts of routine. *It's what I've always done and so it's surely what I must keep doing*, and assume that He's along for the ride. Question marks come knocking at my door, insistent, demanding answers. I reach the horizon of my understanding of Him, and, because I can't figure life out, my fingertips slip off of certainty. In the unknowing, I wonder if He's there. Or His elusiveness frustrates me; I hear no voice, feel no presence, and my requests seemingly go ignored. Is anyone there?

Yes, I know that there's a sense in which I can't lose Him, for the good book says so repeatedly. 'Neither height nor depth, nor anything else in all creation, will be able to separate us from the love of God that is in Christ Jesus' (Rom. 8:39). He's pledged to always be with us, to never forsake us. But that doesn't exclude us from a sense of distance, and, at times, even abandonment. If in doubt, ask the psalmist. My friend, Adrian Plass, remarked that we follow the one who cried, 'My God, my God, why have you forsaken me?' (Matt. 27:46), and that those who follow Him will, at times, feel the same way.

It's a phrase Christians say and sing: 'I've found Jesus', and indeed we have. But in finding Him, I'm still looking for Him, hunting for Him as those anxious parents of His did in the surging crowds of Jerusalem. The book of Revelation declares that one day, in a new Jerusalem, He'll always be located in plain sight, face to face. You won't find Him in the Temple courts (John tells us that there will be no temple in that glorious city) because the Lord God Almighty and the Lamb are the temple. *There He is*. We shall see Him, and we shall be like Him. But in the meantime, the search continues...

14

 Pendulums

It was truly love at first sight. As soon as I set eyes on the beautifully crafted cabinetry of the grandfather clock (and noted the knock-down bargain price), I knew I had to make it mine. The deep-bass boom of the chime and reassuring tick-tock of the 300-year-old timepiece calms my soul. The sound of it accompanied by the smell of blazing logs is surely a perfect Christmas combination, especially if it's chestnuts roasting in that open fire. I'm enamoured with that clock. Whenever I'm tapping away at my keyboard, I am grateful for the sound of it. I am reminded that some things endure, and that not everything that is new is better because of its newness.

Keeping the clock to accurate time, however, has taken some work. Over time, I learnt how to make the tiniest adjustments to the pendulum, a little to the left, a hair to the right, until it was perfectly balanced, accurate to within seconds. Voilà.

Perfectly balanced is how I like to think of myself. In my opinions, my theology, my lifestyle, I try to be balanced. I'm not so sure about everyone else, but I'm centred. My conclusions have been honed and shaped over many years. I ponder them inside my head, listening to myself, and I tend to trust… me. But surely I'm fooling myself.

We're all pendulums and inaccurate ones at that. Our responses are usually in reaction to something, and however much we fool ourselves that we live in the epicentre of correctness, our humanity makes us unreliable. We hold in our hands a Bible that is trustworthy, but the hands that grip the book are not.

Unbalanced pendulums can wreak havoc in the Church. The soul seared by betrayal swings wildly into isolation, quickly growing a thick skin, determined to thwart hurt before it comes knocking. But the reaction caused more pain than the original bruise.

Some people, wearied by ardent prophets who insist that they know the mind of God, react by treating prophecy with contempt. I've done this. I know that God speaks through people – I am in ministry because of a calling confirmed by a reliable, remarkable prophetic voice. But there are some 'prophets' who erode my expectations rather than nurture them. In the early days of the coronavirus pandemic, some 'prophets' lined up to announce the reason for the viral scourge. 'God did it,' they said, 'He wanted to get our attention.' This made me wonder about a God who would use germ warfare to catch our eye. Other insisted that the global illness was the result of God's judgment. Not only was I intrigued by the notion that when bad things happen, God is quickly named as the source, but I also wondered why some of the prophets didn't foresee the coming plague and head us off with a warning. Thus I react, pendulum like.

Rightly angered by bullies thinly disguised as church leaders, there are those who veer into anarchy, insisting that God alone should lead, and thus reject people gifted with true leadership skills. God has always been in the business of raising up servant leaders, and we should not reject His strategy because there are some who sully calling with bullying or abuse.

Others swing wildly out of church altogether, angrily insistent that all that singing, praying and small-grouping are the death-throes of a dying and outmoded institution. In so doing, they deny the truth that God has always had a people, not just persons. Discipleship is not a solo activity but is always about formation flying.

So how can we avoid the extreme pendulum swings?

First, we can start by facing the truth that we're not endlessly and always right. That's difficult because we spend our lives quietly formulating our opinions, rehearsing them to ourselves in that inward conversation called self-talk. We're rather convincing, at least to our own ears and minds. But we are wrong sometimes.

Next, we can get around people who potentially disagree with us and give them permission to speak their mind. Birds of a doctrinal feather tend to flock together, and too often we cocoon ourselves in social circles with like-minded people who heartily endorse *our* views because we confirm the rightness of *their* views. We form a club but it's one that can be collectively wrong because of our mutual backslapping.

Finally, we'd do well to learn to dialogue respectfully and

disagree agreeably. When healthy disagreement descends into lobbing word grenades at each other via the internet, nobody wins. For many Christians, their weapon of choice is a labelling machine. Someone doesn't agree with our cherished view, and we swiftly brand them 'heretic', 'liberal', 'dangerous' or just plain 'wrong'. Let's listen, be patient, see the person and step away from the labelling machine.

Meanwhile, upon hearing the beautiful on-the-hour chimes of my clock, I realise that my ancient timepiece is once again at odds with my more accurate smart watch. Yikes! It's out by a whole three minutes. Perhaps another adjustment is called for. Perhaps it's time for yet another adjustment in *me*.

15

 Billy Graham

It's a description that I've often been tagged with. Evangelist. Much of my ministry has been spent as an itinerant speaker in America, where historically anyone who travelled and preached was thought of as an evangelist. This probably stemmed back to the days when circuit preachers trekked around the wild west on horseback. Fervent and fiery, they shared gospel good news in the hard-drinking, womanising culture where minor conflicts were often settled by a gunfight outside the swing doors of the saloon. I'm not terribly keen on horses, seeing as they don't come equipped with a steering wheel or handbrake. On a recent horse ride, I wasn't able to bring Dobbin to a halt, so I just had to sit tight, while he resolutely trotted back to his stable. And challenged to a gunfight, I'd probably shoot myself in the foot, literally. There were other reasons for my not wanting to be identified as an evangelist. The word has been tarnished, frequently associated with hard sell, dodgy car-salesman types, brash Bible bashers high on volume and low on content. Some evangelists have operated a hit-and-run ministry, mustard keen to see the masses responding, but not as diligent in helping with the follow-up of new converts. Then there's the phrase that really sets my teeth on edge: 'television evangelist'. While all who use television to preach shouldn't be tarred with the same brush, there have been too many who have discredited the office of evangelist with their touch-the-screen approach to healing and their unseemly interest in picking the pockets off their followers. Hearing an announcement from a well-known evangelist who was insisting that his audience provide him with the cash to buy a new private jet (how could he be expected to pray while travelling commercial), I winced, and had yet another of those moments when I felt ashamed to call myself Christian, and even worse to be named as a Christian leader. During the COVID-19 outbreak, that same leading television evangelist 'executed' the virus and declared that its power was over and done. Right, well, that's that then!

I absolutely didn't want to be called an 'evangelist'. But Dr Billy Graham gave dignity to the word. With his lilting North Carolina drawl, he preached with disarming clarity, famously encouraging people to go forward at the end of his services and publicly affirm their faith. His appeal was broad. The Netflix blockbuster *The Crown* featured an episode that portrayed his unique relationship with Queen Elizabeth II. He was also a pastor to 12 presidents, from Harry Truman to Barack Obama. More than that, he was America's pastor, a steadying voice in the dark days following 9/11 and the 1995 Oklahoma bombings, leading memorial services following both tragedies. His gospel was social and for everyone.

At one of his meetings, he removed ropes that had been strung across rows to divide the congregation by race.

Billy Graham is remembered for repeating 'The Bible says...' throughout his sermons. He called millions back to the core narrative of what Tom Wright calls the 'big fat story of God', and to the living Jesus of that story. The late, great John Stott, a personal friend to Billy, once said of him, 'He's a man of the Bible.'

Times have changed. Some might argue that the day for stadium evangelism has now passed. Although our very own fine evangelist, J. John, would disagree and in 2017 held an evangelistic event at the Emirates Stadium where 2,000 people received Christ as their Saviour. Certainly, the terms 'rally' and 'crusade' have less positive interpretations these days but the legacy of Dr William Graham is incalculable. Dying in 2018, he is now reunited with dear Ruth, who went ahead of him after nearly 64 years of marriage.

Thank you, Dr Graham, for a life and ministry that impacted millions. You were the consummate evangelist. And now, at last, you're enjoying your reward. That long battle with Parkinson's disease is over. The Saviour of whom you spoke so eloquently is in plain sight, and heaven is your home. Instead of 'Farewell', we say 'See you in the morning', not with hopeful speculation or vague sentimentality, but because of that oh-so-strong sentence you repeated with such passion.

The Bible says...

16
The folly

It's often called a besetting sin: a sin that an individual constantly struggles with. We're all unique, and so will tend towards differing bad habits or attitudes. Perhaps the writer to the Hebrews had those personal flaws in mind when writing about the 'sin that so easily entangles' (Heb. 12:1). Besetting sins are deep potholes gouged into the pathways of our lives. It's prudent to know where they are and steer around them.

Recently, I did a risk assessment on myself. Looking back over my shoulder, scanning decades as a disciple, I asked the uncomfortable question: *Where am I consistently the weakest?* The list grew alarmingly long. Pride frequently nips at my heels, and I'm prone to allow the stale taste of bitterness to sour my stomach. I don't really struggle with envy – I find it easy to celebrate when others are blessed more than I – but hailing from a cash-starved working-class family means that greed might be an issue. There are others I won't list, to spare you boredom and me embarrassment. But I believe I have identified my premier, besetting sin. It is independence from God.

In my early days, I was obsessed with being in the will of God, and read every book I could find about guidance (having first prayed that I might be in the will of God and find the right book about the will of God). It was agonising as I fretted about whether to shop at Sainsbury's or Tesco, terrified that I might miss the opportunity to talk about Jesus while reaching into the freezer for some fish fingers. It was all rather silly, and bad for my mental health. I felt like I was trying to put together a jigsaw puzzle with 10,000 pieces and terrified that I might fail in the process. And failure might mean – according to my flawed thinking – that I would live a second-best life, disconnected always from God's best. The will of God, in my mind, was a tightrope, with me wobbling away 100 feet up, and with no safety net to catch me. So I did what we often do, I swung away from such neurotic practices, and took my life into my own hands. I talked about pendulums earlier, and this was another one of my reactionary moments.

Taking control and making my own decisions worked out well until my ministry impact began to expand. Opportunities to write and speak multiplied and threatened to paralyse me. So God gave me a clunky reminder to stay close. Attending a Christian leaders' conference, I was invited onstage by Gerald Coates and presented with a bishop's staff, which had previously belonged to Bishop Huddleston who campaigned against apartheid in South Africa.

'Carry the staff with you whenever in ministry,' prophesied Gerald to my chagrin. 'It will be a reminder to depend on God and not on yourself.'

So I did, for a few years.

Some people thought I was mad, others a bit pretentious. Finally, the staff got lost in the bowels of a United Airlines baggage hold, and I thanked God... and forgot the lesson. Slowly, imperceptibly, the tentacles of independence from God began to wrap around me again.

We'd experienced some minor successes in buying and selling property – nothing to make Lord Sugar nervous – so we decided, together with some partners, to build a custom home on an empty plot next to our own house. We'd sell it and make a tidy profit. Kay didn't want to do it and said so. I didn't take time to prayerfully reflect, instead convinced her to come along for the ride, and just rushed ahead. We completed the house just before the housing market crashed. After ten painful years, we sold it – for half the amount we invested in it. Now, because it's next door, every time I come home, I see a monument to my foolishness. It is my folly, and one I will pay for many years to come.

One definition of a folly is a costly ornamental building with no practical purpose, especially a tower or mock-Gothic ruin built in a large garden or park. Technically, the house next door is not a folly because the people who live in it love it. But it is a folly to me. It was created when I ran ahead of God, ignored wise counsel and now it stands as a substantial, permanent reminder of my hurried decision.

Independence is a subtle sin but one that the Bible confronts. In his hard-hitting epistle, James rebukes those who live lives not fully given over to Christ, and ignore the purposes of God as they make choices and decisions. 'Now listen, you who say, "Today or tomorrow we will go to this or that city, spend a year there, carry on business and make money." Why, you do not even know what will happen tomorrow' (James 4:13–14). It's all too possible, having given our lives to Jesus, to slowly, gradually take them back again.

In my case, carting a clunky staff around wasn't enough to rid me of my besetting independent sin. It took a whole, unsold house to get this message into my thick head and sometimes hard heart. Without Jesus, we can do nothing, but sometimes we still try. So let this be our prayer: Lord Jesus, stay close, especially when an opportunity to become independent from You beckons. Amen. And Amen.

17
All grown up

As he came striding towards me, I sighed, resigned to what was to come. It was time for my weekly rebuke. When he'd started attending our church, I'd initially been impressed. He certainly knew his Bible well, and his conversation was liberally sprinkled with quotes from classic Christian books. He faithfully attended our early morning prayer meeting, held at an hour when angels were probably still sleeping. But as time went on, I noticed some worrying trends developing. Undeniably passionate about his faith, that passion morphed into rather unnerving intensity. Ill at ease with laughter, the furrows on his brow deepened because, for him, any fun was frivolous. He eagerly lamented what he viewed as lukewarm spirituality of those who didn't show up to the prayer meeting. His body language was a chilling reflection of an increasingly superior attitude. He'd sit with arms folded tight through my sermon; his posture screaming 'I'm getting nothing out of this' and 'This teaching isn't sound.' Those locked arms only unfolded when he furiously scribbled notes, which were then used as evidence for the prosecution when confronting me with what I should and shouldn't have said. Mostly I was regaled with his demand that the teaching be *deeper*. To this day, I flinch when I hear that 'deep' word in church. Teaching needs to have substance, but some Christians think teaching is only deep if they don't understand a word of it; they beatify bewilderment.

Not much more than 30 years old, he insisted on wearing a suit to church on Sundays. That wasn't a fashion choice, he took the view that he needed to look smart when going to the house of God, which, of course, he was not. God no longer lives in a temple made by human hands, but dwells in human beings and in the midst of His people, the worldwide Church. But our man was convinced that his besuited attire was the only way. It would not have been so bad if he accepted that dressing up was just his personal choice, but he became irritated when others came casually in jeans and T-shirts.

To his credit, he was a keen evangelist, and spent many hours going from door to door, eager to take the gospel to whoever would chat for a while. But after a while, he became frustrated that others didn't feel the same passion or employ his methods.

Armed and dangerous with his notebook, I felt a mixture of sadness and aversion as he approached. His faith seemed to strangle him like his severely knotted tie. Definitely, I didn't want to be like him. He was such a contrast to the newer Christians in our church, with their unspoiled simplicity and openness.

He rebuked me for mispronouncing a Greek word during my sermon and added that he felt that one of the songs we'd sung had given him some theological concerns. I apologised for my mispronunciation, and said I'd ponder the words of the song. Temporarily satisfied, he marched away, unable to control the smirk that had taken over his face. He'd put me in my place, and apparently, that felt good.

It gives me no pleasure to report that tragically he eventually abandoned his faith altogether, a victim of his own black-and-white thinking. His anger towards other Christians, frustrated because they didn't express faith in the same way as he did, ultimately settled as bitterness and rage. He walked away from his marriage, and very loudly renounced his faith. He is still as absolute in his 'non-faith' as ever, refusing to have anything to do with Christianity or Christians.

We Christians crave spiritual maturity, and rightly so. As a new believer, I found myself surrounded by beautiful, older, seasoned souls who had weathered countless storms. Their wisdom was winsome, their smiles warm, and I so wanted to be like them. Of course, there were other crusty, finger-pointers who demonstrated the truth that being long in the tooth doesn't guarantee tenderness of heart but they were the exception. Although faith was so new to me, I quickly discovered the biblical call to maturity, that we all grow up in Christ.

Looking back on my trek towards maturity, I confess that my progress in personal growth has been mixed, to say the least. I envy those disciplined saints who briskly march up the mountain of maturity with barely a break in their step. My own Christian walk has been more of a stagger. Over 40 years on, I still fall asleep when I pray, occasionally wonder if there's even anyone to pray to, and, like an adolescent fighting pimples, I experience sudden outbreaks of immaturity for which there is no cream.

However, I also realised early on the uncomfortable truth that walking the Christian pathway for a good while doesn't mean that you'll be good company, or for that matter, a well-rounded, loving person. If in doubt, consider the Pharisees. A pack of zealots, who prayed for three hours a day, were able to blether on endlessly about minutiae, yet had great talent for noticing gnats and swallowing camels (Matt. 23:24). Rather than forming a coalition with the Pharisees, Jesus reserved His strongest words for them.

As Eugene Peterson puts it, 'The greatest errors in the spiritual life are committed by those who are adept at the spiritual life. The greatest capacity for self-deceit in prayer comes not in the early years, but in the middle and late years.'[1]

I have much to learn, but this much I know. When asked what I want to be when I'm all grown up, I'd like to be a person who ignites a smile rather than a sigh when I approach. I want to be the old guy who is kind, frequently laughs out loud and carries a bag full of chocolate treats for those lovely children in Junior Church. Come to think of it, I'd like to be more like those giggling little ones: childlike, but not childish; silly, but no fool; still thrilled by grace and gracious with it too.

18 In defence of lemmings

It happened in the shoe shop. And then again in a pub where we'd stopped for lunch. And yet again in a local convenience store. In fact, it happened, without fail, no less than six times in one week. Picture the scene. I walk up to the bar or counter, and the person who is serving uses the same sentence, like a mantra that's been agreed upon by retailers everywhere. They could greet customers with a smiley, 'Can I help you?', or 'Hello, what can I get for you?' But no. Those were sentences from more pleasant retail experiences of yesteryear. Now, the standard greeting goes like this: 'You alright there?'

What? For one thing, I'm looking for a coffee, not an opportunity to tell you if I'm alright or not. And secondly, in what specific sense are you enquiring as to my being alright? Would you like to know my mood, blood pressure, BMI or how my recovery is going from a minor surgery completed some 18 months ago? 'You alright there?', I am asked. Am I alright... *where*?

Perhaps it's my popping in and out of the UK, which makes me notice these things. Another phrase I used to hear endlessly was 'I'll tell you what…' before every pronouncement. Simon Cowell frequently uses this verbal preface before he tells a singer something, instead of just saying it! 'Simon Says' is an old game, but when Simon Cowell says something, and a few other celebs adopt the turn of phrase, before long it spreads like an unwelcome rash. This is surely because we humans are creatures that herd. How quickly we emulate those we admire and imitate those who are famous! We copy.

Rather obviously, the fashion industry knows this. We buy what's hot because someone, somewhere decides it's hot. Sometimes this verges on the ridiculous, as the practice known as 'sagging' demonstrates. Some think that this trend, popularised by hip-hop artists in general and Justin Bieber specifically, originated from prison inmates being denied their belts to reduce risk of suicide. Lemming-like, we mindlessly follow. (When I say 'we', I don't mean me. I always wear a belt.)

In recent years, following the crowd has become a very serious issue. Those who want to lead us over a cliff often insist that they are the *only* ones who are right, and we disagree with the crowd at our peril. Liberal fundamentalism rules. If I disagree with the popular consensus, then I'm quickly tagged as 'hateful' or 'bigoted' or 'one who must be silenced and banished immediately'. It's ironic because if we differ in our convictions and opinions, we're accused of being intolerant – and that won't be tolerated.

Christians are called to be non-conformists, regardless of which denominational club we play for. That doesn't mean that we need to be like those who delight in disagreeing and reply 'Yes, but...' to whatever anyone says, thrilled at any opportunity to differ and bring correction.

It's not so much that we need to be original, but rather follow the ultimate original, Jesus. He consistently walked out of step with the religious and social norms of the day. The Pharisees demanded that He conform and condemned Him with the shrill tones peculiar to the religious. But they couldn't cramp His style as He lunched with outcasts, touched lepers and toppled rip-off Temple tables. If we are to walk in His footsteps, there will surely be times when faithfulness calls us to take an unpopular road.

I mentioned lemmings earlier, famous for hurtling over cliffs in large numbers in a mindless suicide pact. But apparently there is some reasoning behind the free falling. Lemmings have population explosions every three or four years, and when that happens, a large group will set out in search of a new home. Able to swim, if they reach a water obstacle, such as a river or lake, they may try to cross it. Inevitably, a few individuals drown. It's hardly suicide but the idea persists, helped along by Hollywood. In the 1958 Disney nature film, *White Wilderness*, filmmakers staged a lemming death plunge, pushing dozens of lemmings off a cliff as the cameras rolled. The images wrongly convinced several generations of moviegoers that these little rodents do, in fact, possess a bizarre instinct to destroy themselves. In fact, lemmings take the plunge because they are in search of a new home. There's a reason for their high diving.

We humans often have no reason at all for our herd-like

behaviour. We get in step with everyone else simply because everyone else is marching in that direction and forget that the crowd isn't always right.

Let's keep our eyes on Jesus and follow Him. He'll lead us on the right path.

As for me. Am I alright there? I'll tell you what... I'm alright, thank you.

19
Open to suggestions

I had a feeling that it would be a disaster. Perhaps inspired by too many episodes of *Strictly Come Dancing*, Kay suggested that it would be fun to attend a ballroom dancing class. I smiled thinly, thinking that this would be about as fun as a colonic procedure, but eager to please. My confidence was low, mainly because I'm not too good at coordinating my limbs with my brain. (Recent attempts at skiing confirmed this: my attempts at smooth navigation of the slopes resulted in what can best be described as a downhill spasm.) My fears were quickly confirmed. An hour into the class, other couples were looking positively fluid compared to my robotic staggering; it seemed that my objective was to bruise every single one of Kay's toes. It was not going well. But then things went from bad to worse as the instructor hissed in my ear, 'Lead, Jeff, for goodness sake, take the lead.' He strongly encouraged me, as the male partner, to initiate the steps with confidence. I had to lead the way.

The call of Jesus always begins with following. He's the boss. That's sometimes easy to forget. I mentioned earlier that we can give our lives to Jesus, only to gradually, incrementally, take them back again. But when we look at the Gospels, we discover that He's also open to suggestions, for us to initiate occasionally, take a lead now and then. I've written about this before, but it's worth another visit.

Maybe you're not convinced that God is open to suggestions? Peter's famous walk on the turbulent waters of the Sea of Galilee began, not with Jesus coming up with the idea, but Peter suggesting it. Granted, Peter waited for Jesus' approval of the notion: 'Lord, if it's you... tell me to come to you on the water' (Matt. 14:28). But it was still Peter's idea, one that Jesus agreed to. An even more radical example is found at the beginning of Jesus' ministry when, as a wedding guest at Cana, the wine ran out, which was more than a minor problem.

Jesus' mother, Mary, was known to be pushy at times (she tried to organise a family intervention and forcibly take Jesus back to His home village, so concerned was she about His mental health, Mark 3:21). She knew of a solution to the wine shortage problem. To the servants, she said, 'Do whatever he tells you' (John 2:5). Initially, Jesus objected, insisting that the time for miracles was not yet at hand but He conceded. The first miracle of His ministry was not just someone else's idea but the result of parental pressure.

Not every idea offered to Jesus met with His approval – James and John learnt that when they angrily wanted to nuke a Samaritan village (Luke 9:54). Peter also found himself on the receiving end of a stinging rebuke when suggesting that, for Jesus, the cross was not a good idea (Matt. 16:22). Other suggestions from the disciples also received the thumbs down; for example, when they tried to dismiss the parents of the children brought to Jesus for blessing (Matt. 19:13). Another time, when a woman gave an extravagant gift of perfume to Jesus, the disciples wrinkled their noses at her gesture and made somewhat hollow speeches about the poor (Matt. 26:8–9). Jesus silenced their objections and their verbal attack on the woman without hesitation.

So not every idea was adopted but that said, let's realise that God is open to suggestions. Abraham had a lengthy session of negotiation with God. Trying to make a deal for Sodom and Gomorrah, Abraham succeeded in nudging God to relent, to change His mind (Gen. 18:16–33). Some theologians and commentators choke at this. But what is prayer if it does not include the offering of suggestions to God as we present our requests?

At Timberline Church, where I serve as a teaching pastor, we invited team leaders to give five-minute talks and share their wildest dreams, not just for their teams, but for the whole church. We then gathered up our armfuls of dreams and offered them to Jesus – whose church it is.

Meanwhile back on the dance floor, my attempts at leading failed dismally and we finally gave up, mainly because Kay values her feet. I came away feeling like a clumsy clod – a sense that I frequently experience. But I'd like to be a little more tenacious in prayer and include some bold requests. Who knows? Fine wine and water-walking just might result.

20

 In praise of creativity

I met him at the end of an evening of theatre, music and teaching. I'm no thespian, but have spent a fair amount of time trekking around the world with my pals from Searchlight Theatre Company and also with the much-loved Adrian Plass, presenting creative evenings designed to make people laugh, cry and think. The unplanned nature of some of these on-stage events has led to moments of mild panic and terror, but joy and laughter too. People have seemingly enjoyed an alternative and hopefully entertaining way to explore truth.

The Searchlight evening had gone well, the audience appreciative, and I was risking a feeling of mild encouragement as the crowds dispersed and we broke down the set and began to haul it out to the van. It was then that the man sidled up alongside me. He said he had a question, which he did not. It was a statement thinly disguised as an enquiry, and he was not looking for any answers. 'I don't get it, Jeff. What's the point of all this drama, humour and music? Surely the main task of the Church is to preach the Word of God? I can't find entertainment in the Bible, you know. Come to think of it, I can't find creativity either.' I stifled a cough – it was better than loud screaming. I so wanted to deliver a seminar on the power of humour. (Little children loved Jesus; they would have run a mile from a wide-eyed straight-faced odd bloke.)

When it comes to creativity, the Bible is loaded with it. It all starts with 'In the beginning, God created' (Gen. 1:1) and continues throughout the book with the priests dressing up in their fancy costumes, sharing mini-dramas to remind forgetful Israel of her history; with the architects and builders shaping tents and buildings; with Jesus telling little stories to spark imagination; with John on Patmos laying out a Spirit-inspired poem to announce that, in the end, God wins. Creativity is everywhere in Scripture.

Sadly, even though progress has been made, we, the Church, have not always empowered or valued the creatives. In a culture dominated by words, all too often the poets, dancers, actors, sculptors and artists have felt sidelined. Musicians have usually fared better, but those from other disciplines have often been left behind. Those in Christian leadership surely need to ask: Is what we do together as a church a rounded reflection of the God who played with palettes of colour, crafting scrawny giraffes, boggled-eyed deep-sea fish with ridiculous antennae, technicolor peacocks and intricate bugs so small only the creator Himself can see them?

These reflections present an ideal opportunity for me to celebrate and give thanks for the brilliance of a man whose work has graced my magazine columns for a few years now.

Noel Ford, an award-winning cartoonist, provided visuals that powerfully amplified the message that I'd shaped in words. Noel has had the uncanny knack of capturing the key thought, and then expressing that thought with great artwork that at times made me laugh out loud. His has been a rare gift. In 2019, this doodling genius passed away. We give thanks to God for Noel's creative talent. He will be much missed. But while Noel's passing nudges me to pay tribute, and rightly so, it also reminds me to include and empower those in our churches who can dance and paint and act and rap the message. How tragic would it be if we ignored and neglected the gifts that God has granted them?

I never did manage to convince the grumbling chap that creativity was an expression of the truth that the universe is governed by an artist. He had already made up his mind. I felt the creeping despair that comes when we have worked hard, only to have our efforts trashed by a few acerbic words of disdain. I gave up the discussion and asked if he would help us pack the scenery into the van. He declined.

21
 Risen for us

The restaurant was heaving with post-church diners. I scanned the throng, looking for Kay who had gone ahead to secure a table.

I had enjoyed church. Mostly. The Easter Sunday morning service is usually my favourite but when we shared the traditional resurrection greeting, a niggle surfaced in my heart. The smiling pastor exclaimed, 'The Lord is risen!' and, on cue, the congregation joyfully replied, 'He is risen indeed!' As I joined in with the expected response, I sensed the faintest hint of a question mark, but I couldn't think why.

I *do* believe that Jesus is alive, right now, despite it being entirely impossible for a man dead three days to neatly fold His own shroud and walk out into the sunlight. But with God all things are possible. No, this was not an attack of raw doubt, but something more subtle.

Brushing the niggle aside like a pesky mosquito, it was then that I saw them, a crowded table of ten, waving at me, inviting me to come over. As one of the pastoral staff of a church of thousands in a relatively small city, this often happens. I bump into people who know me because they see me on a platform, but I don't know them.

I strolled over to their table. 'Hi everyone! Happy Easter! How are you?'

They nodded, smiled, said they were fine, and I launched into some fairly nondescript chatter. They joined in, politely, as I blethered on about this and that. But after a minute or three, I sensed yet another niggle: something was amiss here. They were looking nervous. There was some shuffling in their seats. The source of discomfort couldn't be the furniture upholstery. Perhaps I'd overstayed my welcome. It's happened before. And then a more awful thought.

I decided to ask, 'Er... I don't think that you know me, do you?'

One of them, a brave soul, confirmed my worst fear. 'You're right, sir. We've never seen you before in our lives.'

'But you waved me over when I walked in!' I protested.

'We were waving at the chap behind you.'

My face flushed crimson. I wanted the ground to swallow me up. There was nothing else to say but apologise.

'I am so very, very sorry. I'll go away now, forever,' I mumbled, making a hasty retreat.

They were greeting someone else. Not me.

Reflecting later, the episode helped me to identify the source of my Easter mid-service anxiety. Sometimes I worry that something similar will happen when I finally meet Jesus. He'll smile, open His arms wide for a hug, and I'll rush towards Him. But the joy that I feel is suddenly vaporised as He steps back, a look of consternation now on His face.

'I'm sorry...' He says, His eyes sad now. 'I was talking to the person behind you. Not you.'

We can develop the feeling that Jesus loves the *world*, broadly, but not necessarily *us*, personally. What we believe can distill into being just cold theory, like our belief in the existence of the planet Neptune. We know that it's out there but its existence doesn't make any impact on how we think and live. We're left feeling like spectators, outsiders even, when the great truths of the faith are celebrated.

It's easy to feel counted *out* when it comes to blessing and counted *in* when judgment is sounded. If I stood up in church and announced that the Lord had revealed to me that there were some people present who brought special delight to Him because of their good choices, a lot of people would be craning their necks, looking around, wondering who merited such encouragement, but not thinking for a moment that it could be them. Conversely, if I declared that I felt that there were some who had irritated God and should ready themselves for a dose of fire and brimstone, many would rush to think that fireproof underwear might be a wise shopping choice.

The good news of the cross and resurrection is for all of us who often feel like we're on the outside, looking in. A dying thief is promised paradise. Thomas, most famous for his doubting, misses the meeting of his life, but then is treated to another opportunity to encounter the risen Jesus. Peter, foot squarely in his mouth with a fireside denial, is treated to an early-morning fireside breakfast.

Christ *is* risen. He's preparing a place for us. We'll be with Him, and tears, sorrow and death will have all have gone away – forever. The good news is for you. Me. Us.

The Lord is risen. He is risen indeed. Hallelujah!

22

 Losing my voice

It all started when some gremlins visited. While I was sleeping, those bacterial invaders quietly removed the inside lining of my throat and replaced it with sandpaper. A tickle became a cough, and the leading invader – a pesky cold virus – reduced me to a wheezing, watery-eyed, sniffling wreck, box of tissues permanently in hand. I imbibed so many of those lemony hot drinks, I probably smelt like a Spanish orchard. My snoring sounded like a warthog, according to my wife. And while Kay didn't exactly walk around ringing a bell and shouting, 'Unclean! Unclean!', she certainly kept her distance. But one of the worst symptoms of all was the loss of my voice. For someone who preaches a lot, broadcasts on radio, and generally likes to natter to people, this was not good. Parked in bed, stuffed to the gills with legal pharmaceuticals, it occurred to me that, for a couple of decades or so, I have been battling with voice loss, which has nothing to do with my vocal cords.

When I first heard the good news about Jesus and decided to follow Him, I was loud about God. Very loud. With the bellicose hollering of a town-crier, I shared the gospel message with anybody who would listen, and with quite a few who were desperate not to listen. Like an excitable salesperson paid by commission, I viewed anybody in my nearby proximity as a prospect. The mistaken notion that single-handedly one must tell everybody that one meets about Jesus (and be somewhat responsible for their eternal destiny) makes a chap feel a little jumpy. Many of my attempts to share the good news made it sound less than good. Clumsily, I tried to wrench every conversation around to Jesus. 'Hello, would you like a cheese sandwich?' some kind soul would enquire. My grinning response was certainly cheesy: 'No, thank you, I have the bread of life. How about you?' Some people started to avoid me as though I was infectious, and when my 'sharing' became an endless monologue, I'm sure I heard some snoring from others here and there.

Then came the gradual change. I heard someone quoting St Francis of Assisi (famous for chatting with squirrels), 'Preach the Gospel at all times. When necessary, use words.' Unaware that the great man never said that, my voice went quiet. Francis did say, 'All the friars... should preach by their deeds,' and 'There is no use walking anywhere to preach if you're walking isn't your preaching.' He did use words, lots of words. Francis sometimes visited five villages in one day to talk to people about Jesus. But tragically, his famous quotes have been used as an excuse to justify our silence.

Red-faced and head down, I began to hurry past that ranting street preacher with his loud-hailer and 'Repent Now' poster. As he yelled threats at passing shoppers, I decided I wanted to be nothing like him. My voice went quieter still.

Some people teach that our acts of love and service in the community don't always have to be accompanied by gospel explanations. That's certainly true enough. But if we are rendered speechless about the reason for our caring, surely we become a welcome and respected but benign bunch of do-gooders.

The gospel has always been news to both show *and* tell. In Paul's letter to Titus, Paul encourages the church in Crete to live lives that will enhance the gospel: 'so that in every way they will make the teaching about God our Saviour attractive' (Titus 2:10). That doesn't mean that every act of goodness must be accompanied by a proclamation: 'Welcome to the food bank; you must be born again.' But we do need to be 'prepared to give an answer to... the reason for the hope that you have' (1 Pet. 3:15). That does imply that we'll be responding to a question rather than sprinting to an answer where none has been requested, but words will still be needed to give that response. Peter also adds that we need to do this 'with gentleness and respect', so I still won't be joining in with the ranting street preacher.

Nevertheless, the gospel *is* news. We, through words and example, are newscasters, sharers of vital information. Sadly, we don't always do a good job at newscasting. This was illustrated recently during yet another trip through an airport.

I especially dislike the immigration area with those automatic barriers. I worry that a malfunctioning gate might treat me to a free amputation – and I like both my legs.

Approaching the immigration zone in Heathrow airport

recently, I joined the mildly befogged gaggle of bleary-eyed passengers who were sleep deprived from their night flights and perhaps suffering from too much airborne alcohol. Unsure of which lane to choose, I approached a bored-looking chap who was sporting an employee badge. He would be the one to ask, or so I thought. I was so very wrong.

'Am I in the right lane for passport check?' I asked.

'Go, whatever, there, green light,' he mumbled, which did nothing to dispel my confusion.

'Sorry, what did you say?' I ventured hopefully, but in vain.

'Yes, go, stand, wait, no,' he replied, which made me wonder if *he* had been up all night enjoying the fruit of the vine.

Other passengers approached him. He grunted, responding with sentences that were quite incomprehensible. He impatiently waved some on without an answer. One by one people shrugged their shoulders, and shuffled on, none the wiser.

It was then that I noticed that this uncommunicative chap had a huge letter 'i' enclosed in a florescent yellow circle, with the word 'information' underneath, printed on the back of his T-shirt. He is employed for one purpose: to provide information for hapless travellers. Being informative is his job description. But for whatever reason, nobody could extract anything remotely helpful from him.

There are lost people who very much need to be found. They need to be informed about the way to life. Who knows? Perhaps today we might be able to nudge someone towards Christ. But that won't happen if you and I are incoherent, irrelevant or inaudible.

Being informative about Jesus. It's our job description.

In short, I want to get my voice back.

23

 Just do it

I think it's a trait that I inherited from my late mother. I loved her dearly, but she never followed instructions, directions or recipes. When concentrated washing powder first appeared in shops, she fed the washing machine with the same amount of snowy white granules as unconcentrated, resulting in a seriously frothy kitchen with us kids sloshing around in suds up to our armpits. My mother was rather sniffy about recipes too, preferring to trust her own culinary instincts, which would have been fine, had she had any culinary instincts. Some of the dishes she created missed their calling. They were so gut-wrenchingly awful, I thought that they might have been weaponised. Concerns about any foreign military capability would have been resolved easily if my mum had been let loose with a cooker and an apron. The mere threat of her custard would have brought any aggressor to their knees immediately, which would have been great, except that the custard itself would still pose its own nuclear threat.

All of which makes me wonder if my own disdain for directions is inherited. When driving and lost (which happens frequently), and Siri is ignoring me (which has happened a lot this month, I think that she's going through a rough patch), I resort to the ancient practice of pulling over to ask a stranger for some directional assistance. This begins well enough but as they describe the '...fourth turn on the left... after the light... just past the Dog and Duck...', I get bored with listening and switch off, while nodding appreciatively. Perhaps sensing my inattention, the kindly stranger then repeats the entire list of directions again, which again goes in one ear and out the other.

There's more evidence of my disregard for instructions. Recently we purchased a new TV. I asked the salesperson, who was apparently nine years old, if I would be able to set the TV up without assistance. 'Sir, of course!' replied the grinning preadolescent, and then added, 'Any idiot could set this TV up.' Tossing the instructions aside, in this case because they were written by someone for whom English is a second language, I struggled for three hours, pausing occasionally for seasons of muttering. What did I mutter? It was, 'Oh Hallelujah!' Or something like that. I'm not just any idiot, it seems, I'm a total idiot.

All of this has led me to consider breaking the genealogical chain by taking up reading, digesting and following instructions. That resolve could apply to life more broadly. The Bible is loaded with wisdom provided by God for our direction, and not just as fodder to enlarge our information banks.

Following directions requires humility. The starting point is the acknowledgement of our need for God's help. Followed by a readiness to respond and obey. As veteran American broadcaster Ted Koppel wisely mused, 'What Moses brought down from Mount Sinai were not ten suggestions. They are Commandments.' When it comes to following instructions, don't be like my mother; follow the advice of Jesus' mother instead. To the servants at a wedding in Cana, Mary said: 'Do whatever he tells you' (John 2:5).

Sadly, my commitment to read and obey instructions has been rather short-lived. Recently we brought an item of furniture, a cupboard, which required self-assembly. True to form, I ignored the instructions, but triumphantly completed the assembly in record time for me, just two hours of sweat and muttering instead of the usual three. And I'm pleased to report that I only had just one minor item left over when the assembling was complete.

It was a door.

24

 Name calling

Political developments often provide the world with an interesting cast of characters, from US presidents to UK prime ministers to those in leadership around the globe. For a start, certain world leaders seem to have very odd hairstyles, causing hairdressers worldwide to reach for their scissors, itching to give these headline grabbers a decent trim. But without even getting into any party-political issues, there are other, more serious, concerns.

The way that conflict is handled these days is often a worry. It is very easy for individuals to fire off a tweet labelling prominent figures as 'stupid', 'sleazy' or 'bimbo'. One UK prime minister famously called his colleagues in the London Assembly 'great supine protoplasmic invertebrate jellies', which although creative was very acerbic.

The political arena has always been a place of fierce argument and fast retort. Sir Winston Churchill, rightly celebrated for oratory that galvanised a nation at war, knew the power of an acidic sentence. 'I wish Stanley Baldwin no ill, but it would have been much better if he had never lived,' he said in 1946. He called Labour leader Ramsay MacDonald 'a sheep in sheep's clothing'. On Prime Minister Clement Attlee, he mused, 'There is less there than meets the eye.'

Sometimes vitriol can worryingly plummet new depths. Instead of debating issues, leaders resort to infantile barbs and personal attacks. Sadly, when adults in high office model bullying behaviour, young people may well feel justified in doing the same.

We Christians need to beware too. As said before, a favoured weapon of choice among believers is the labelling machine. A Christian leader raises genuine concerns and questions about a topic and is quickly tagged as a 'heretic'. There *is* such a thing as heresy and truth must be guarded, but it's the speed at which the label is applied that's worrying. Those in leadership can be guilty of labelling too, especially the more insecure types. As a young pastor, I was irritated by a lady in our church who fearlessly confronted the male-dominated model of leadership that we had. I quickly tagged her as 'divisive' and viewed her as an interloper who threatened our unity. However, she was perfectly within her rights to raise her concerns, and I'm grateful that she accepted my apology some years later.

There is a genre of name-calling, which is particularly devastating because the person attacked has no means of defence. A preacher is dubbed as 'unsound'. Their teaching is not 'deep enough' – an entirely subjective accusation because there's no way to scientifically measure just what is 'deep enough'. Exuberant worship is sniffly dismissed as 'frothy'. Healthy discussion and disagreement become impossible, while dissidents are tagged as 'traitors'.

Authentic unity is not the result of an absence of conflict. If you're in a church where everyone always agrees on everything, and dissenters are quickly shuffled to the edges, then run for your life; the doctrine may be orthodox, but you might be unwittingly trapped in something that has the social structure of a cult.

Not only is all this name-calling hurtful, but ironically, it doesn't help us get to the truth. When we lob verbal grenades at each other, and then duck in the trenches with others who share our opinions and prejudices, we won't grow. Name-calling is lazy; it's easy to smear and demean those who disagree with us with a well-aimed insult rather than rigorously engage with their argument.

So next time we find ourselves in a cauldron of conflict, let's play nicely, and disagree agreeably. And if you are a little offended at my earlier tongue-in-cheek comments about the hairstyles of certain world leaders, just call me stupid and superficial. Or maybe... don't.

25
 Easily offended

As I write, I am offended. Travelling by train to London, I've decided to make the best use of time and write this chapter. I've placed my laptop on the table – a table designed to be shared, hence the source of my ire. The man sitting opposite me is taking up about 60% of the table space, leaving just 40% for me. I am quietly outraged. But there's more, because now this brazen table-hogger has placed a steaming hot cup of coffee on the table as well, taking up yet more space (I calculate about 67%) and risking third-degree burns to yours truly if the juddering train should topple it. I begin to plan for that toppling, mentally rehearsing a withering speech should I end up being scalded. You could say that I'm 'prophetically offended' – planning a retort should something (highly unlikely) happen. I am disgusted to admit that I am almost eager for a valid opportunity to complain, even if it involves minor burns.

I don't think I'm alone in my bristling: it seems like we are a culture that has perfected the art of being offended. Earlier, I wrote about the concerning way that our politicians and leaders often descend into acerbic jibing. Yet ironically, surely our verbosity is perhaps only matched by our fragility.

Gary Lineker (he of footie and crisps fame) made a 'hair-raising' joke at the expense of his bald co-presenters (who found it amusing) only to discover that complaints were made. The overreaction to this harmless joshing was staggering (and I say that as one with a hairstyle that is a shrinking peninsula). Another time, an American TV host reported that young Prince George had taken up ballet and suggested that his interest in dance might not last long, which triggered rage among ballet-lovers everywhere. They demanded an apology and suggested that the host was guilty of bullying. Opinions may differ about the wisdom of her comment, but perhaps those who suggest that we are becoming a 'snowflake' society where everyone is perpetually offended might have a point.

While we do need to call out the occasions when celebrities, politicians or journalists make tasteless comments, there is the danger of taking things too far. Some people seem to live their entire lives permanently camped on the brink of being offended. They probably got upset with the midwife who delivered them, irritated to leave the comfort of their mother's womb.

Offence can be weaponised. It can be used as a nifty ruse. Instead of angrily stamping feet and huffing and puffing, some people employ the trembling bottom lip routine, causing others to quickly attempt to appease them. The aggrieved victim manages to become the victor by manipulating the situation.

Christians have an extra weapon that can upgrade a pop gun of offence into the relational equivalent of something nuclear: God. Upset at the sermon / worship song / service time / pew arrangement / not being included in the flower rota (if you love being offended, join a church – there's no shortage of issues that can irritate), we insist that our preference or opinion mirrors God's view on the matter. The Lord of the cosmos is called as a witness for our prosecution.

Meanwhile, the chap sitting opposite me on the train has finished his coffee, so I am denied the opportunity to be scalded and thus be scalding, but he is inching his laptop yet further into my already minuscule table territory. I might have to have a word, just as soon as I've finished this chapter. Which is now…

Having just re-read the chapter, I am staying quiet. Scalding unlikely.

26

 Seeing people

Once on my travels, I almost got into a fight, and I'm not talking about a war of words. I met a thoroughly unpleasant chap, and it almost came to blows. I know. It's a bit odd for a Christian minister to confess that he came close to a punch-up. As soon as it happened, I knew I had to share the experience. But before you read on, let me issue a health warning: I am about to introduce you to a real-life nasty piece of work.

Kay and I were at Chicago airport, waiting for our flight. The departure lounge was packed; the atmosphere dank with the mild despair that descends when multiple flights are delayed due to weather. Everyone hopefully – and occasionally hopelessly – stared at the departure boards. Peckish, we entered a teeming restaurant and found the last two chairs at a shared table. Across from us, a very expensive-looking bag, all fur and leather, occupied a seat. We assumed it belonged to a man who sat next to it, but we were wrong.

An older lady came by and enquired about the bag. 'Is this yours?' she asked, ever so sweetly.

Nobody around the table claimed ownership. It was then that the winner of 'rudest man of my lifetime' award made himself known. He was young, handsome and dressed in designer clothing with flashy jewellery. Sitting up at a bar just across from the table, he barked, 'That's my bag. I don't want it on the floor, so leave it alone. When I've finished my meal, I'll move it.'

Mouths opened around the table, aghast at the suggestion that this elderly lady be made to stand while this posh but inanimate object occupied the only available chair. This was absurd, rude, crass.

I decided to take action, and – perhaps a little louder than necessary – invited the lady to take my chair. She sat down, then smiled and whispered, 'Perhaps you could teach him a lesson.'

Emboldened by her encouragement, I walked over and gently tapped Mr Rude on the shoulder. 'Excuse me, sir, but have I understood? You want this lovely lady to stand and wait while you eat, because your luggage is that important?' I confess to feeling a little heroic in that moment.

He glared back at me, his deep-blue eyes cold. Then he snapped back, his thin lips tight. 'Now look here, it seems that you're the gentleman, and you gave her your seat, so it's good. Yes?'

That's when I knew we were at a point of no return. His icy stare made his message clear: just say one more word and I'm going to hit you. I decided not to say one more word for a number of reasons:

   (a) I'm allergic to pain;

   (b) it's awkward when ministers get into an airport fracas

and are then arrested; and

(c) I felt like my job had been done.

Call me a coward, and you might well be right.

Back at the table, we chatted happily with the older lady. Eventually, young bag-obsessed blue-eyes stopped by to pick up his priceless luggage, and with a rude parting shot, he headed out to catch his flight. I spent the rest of the day internally fuming about his staggering gift of arrogance. Our flight was delayed further, so I wandered around the airport, hoping to see him, to pursue our chat a little. Providentially, I didn't find him.

Obviously, the rude man's attitude was a somewhat extreme, but I wonder how often I am just like him. In that moment, he failed to see a person, that lady who needed a chair. And we can do the same thing, especially if we deal with people a lot. The busy doctor in the casualty ward is told that there's a broken arm in cubicle six, rather than recently widowed Mr Jones has had a nasty fall. The shop assistant yawns, indifferent to the customer who has become just another commodity. The pastor looks out over the congregation, seeing a crowd, recording Sunday morning attendance numbers and offering figures, not noticing real flesh-and-blood people with hopes, dreams, needs and heartaches. The hunched figure wrapped in a thin sleeping bag in a doorway becomes a homeless statistic rather than a person with a name and a story. The great Jewish theologian Martin Buber spoke of our dangerous temptation to treat people as objects rather than subjects.

All around us today are people – unique, needy, hopeful, hopeless, fascinating people. Let's notice them.

27

 Keep calm and pray

Odd things happen when people are baptised by full immersion. I know a minister who wore fisherman's waders so that he wouldn't have to change clothing for the event. The waders leaked, and he became one waterlogged pastor, which was awkward. Another hapless besuited leader delegated the actual baptising to one of his team but popped onto the platform to provide a benediction at the end of the service – and then stepped back into the tank. Oh dear.

I mentioned earlier that my own baptism was something of a fiasco. Baptismal candidates were expected to share a testimony prior to the dunking, so I decided to write and perform a song – a huge mistake. Singing a duet with a friend, we tortured the fixed-grinned congregation with our awful verses. Then, as I shared earlier, when submerged, I kicked my legs up in the air, sending a miniature tidal wave towards the elderly ladies on the front pew.

But my most recent baptismal experience was epically aquatic. Visiting the Holy Land during one of our annual tours, there were 32 members of our group who wanted to be baptised in the River Jordan. The site is allegedly the place where Jesus was baptised by John. We're not precious about these things on our tours; we don't offer 'See where Moses had a cappuccino' excursions. Nevertheless, being baptised in same vicinity as Jesus is special. And challenging.

At the baptismal site, the River Jordan is about 10 metres wide at most, and the border between Israel and the nation of Jordan is a rope right in the centre of the river. On each bank, Jordanian and Israeli border guards usually stand, machine guns in hand – a warm and comforting sight.

All was going well until our friend Gerry waded into the water. My wife Kay and I gulped. Gerry is a tall chap, and the river current was strong, so baptising him might take a little extra effort. We meant to ease him back into the water slowly, carefully. But in his enthusiasm, he threw himself backwards, emigrating in the process. For a moment, his head was in the nation of Jordan, his nether regions in Israel. The guards moved closer. This could create an international incident. I didn't immediately see those guards because I was totally underwater, thrown off-balance by his sudden backflip. Flailing around, I surfaced to witness our compassionate group laughing hysterically at the sight of our mass immersion. Why did this happen? Simple. Kay and I had not planted our feet firmly on the riverbed, and thus we were vulnerable. We were not standing securely.

Staying still for most people doesn't seem too exciting.

The activists' mantra mocks the apparent inactivity with a call to perpetual motion: 'Don't just stand there, do something.' But sometimes staying in one place is all we're called to do, because there's nothing else to be done. We've come to an impassable junction. We've tried all the usual things. We've prayed, consulted, worked and planned. We've even exhausted a few useless options too, like fretting and worrying. And now we're facing a concrete wall of our own limitations, and all we can do is stop and trust.

Again, I write this during the early days of the coronavirus pandemic. We've often used the phrase, 'We don't know what on earth is going on', but right now, quite literally, we don't know what on earth is going on. People are sick and dying all around the globe. The world's economies are struggling in the fight against this dreaded plague. Sadly, some believers, in their rush to understand why this pandemic has happened, have reached some ridiculous conclusions. One 'prophet' suggested that the whole thing is a ruse, a conspiracy to lull us all into submitting to a new world order. I couldn't watch the rest of his broadcast. It made me nauseous.

When we don't know the 'why', and we're not sure about the 'what', what we can do is pray. Wait. Reflect. Calm our hearts. Hold our nerve. In short, keep firm.

We're also called to 'stand firm' when spiritual warfare rages. Writing to some battle-weary believers in Ephesus, Paul encouraged them to clothe themselves, not with leaky waders, but with the 'full armour of God, so that when the day of evil comes, you may be able to stand your ground, and after you have done everything, to stand' (Eph. 6:13).

We have assurance about what is true. It was Paul again who told those endlessly wobbly souls in Corinth, famous for their doctrinal vacillations, to hold tightly to the truth that Christ is raised from the dead (1 Cor. 15:1–7). Because of that wondrous Easter dawn, death is dead to us too.

So here are a few words of advice. Don't be swayed. Hold tightly to what you believe. Don't be intimidated or swept away by uncertainty. And if you're planning a baptism in a river, keep your balance.

28

On edge with Jesus

We were young and foolish – at least that's my excuse and I'm sticking to it. A gaggle of fresh-faced Bible college students, sharing a six-person dormitory, we were all very passionate about our faith, rather convinced that we had what it took to change the world by next Thursday – which we did not. We got along, mostly, although there was one occasion when two of our number almost got into a fist fight over Calvinism versus Arminianism. Hostilities ceased short of an actual punch-up, although I think that the Calvinist would have triumphed because he felt that everything, including his victory, was eternally predetermined.

One of our number had two memorable characteristics. One was a deafening snore. Many nights we were awakened by what sounded like a mud-basking rhino in our room, which caused much frustration. Those kept awake wrestled with, but thankfully resisted, the temptation to smother him with a pillow. His other trait was a deep-seated fear that God was going to commission him to be a missionary to some far-flung corner of the globe. He talked endlessly about his worry. His nervousness heightened as each weekly chapel service approached – the likely zone for a calling from God to land – and if the chapel speaker was a missionary, his fear factor shot through the roof. He talked about his phobia a great deal, and so one night, when his snoring sounded like a Harley-Davidson revving up in our room, we decided to play a little trick. He was in deep sleep as we gathered around his bed. For about ten minutes, the five of us whispered the same sentence over and over: 'Go to the mission field, go to the mission field…' Our hope was that the repetition would seep into his subconsciousness, and we were not disappointed.

The next morning, the words having penetrated his head, he was in a panic meltdown. 'Guys! Last night I heard voices speaking to me. I think the calling is actually happening. This is terrible!' We stayed silent and let him suffer. Payback for our insomnia. You might think that our little joke was rather cruel, but then you didn't have to share a room with a large revving motorcycle.

Our room-mate's concern points to a very real problem: how many of us Christians say that we love Jesus, but offering our lives to Him makes us feel continuously uneasy and on edge? It certainly did for me in my early days as a follower. Someone remarked that the will of God was probably the opposite of what we might want to do – an idea that portrays God as one who delights in dreaming up plans for us that we would find unpalatable. This concerned me greatly as I was going out with a very attractive young lady whom I loved. If

God's will for me was *not* what I wanted, then did the Lord want me to abandon her? This warped thinking nearly cost me the relationship that has led to a 42-year marriage.

Some Christians are insecure about their salvation, and worry that, when they finally get to see Jesus face to face in heaven, they will be met with a glare rather than a smile. Instead of being at peace in the knowledge of God's grace and forgiveness, they feel the need to pay for their sins daily with good works. It's hard to be at rest when your view of God is a hard-to-please taskmaster.

God may well call us to do the difficult, the awkward, or even, as our brothers and sisters in the persecuted Church know all too well, follow a pathway that leads to prison or death. We're not promised an easy ride. But let's know that, whatever we're called to, we are utterly loved by Him, totally secure in Him, and that what He does for and with us is rooted in His stunning kindness and grace.

And that snoring, reluctant missionary from our dormitory? Despite his calling coming from a giggling, whispering group around his bedside, he has served with distinction and success as a missionary for the last 40 years, planting many churches and opening schools in remote areas.

No, I'm just kidding. We told him about the trick that we'd played on him later that day. He never did get a missionary calling.

But this much *is* true: God's love us for us is perfect, and we are invited to rest easy in that love. And that's a calling that is very, very real.

29

 The new normal

It happened decades ago, and even though I have spent a lifetime navigating through one embarrassing situation to another, I still blush at the memory.

As a student in Bible college, I went to the gym for a workout and a sauna. It was a respectable leisure centre run by the town council. Wednesday was men only day in the sauna. I collected my towel from an attractive young lady in the reception area, and proceeded into the sauna area, which was filled with naked chaps. I was momentarily startled by a rather obese gentlemen who came flying out of the sauna room at speed, his skin lobster red. I undressed and headed for the showers. There were no cubicles, just shower heads jutting out of the wall. I was facing forward, staring at the white tiles, the hot water cascading over me, when I heard the voice.

'Is it your first time here?' As I turned around to face the enquirer, it occurred to me that this was a female voice. And indeed, it was. The smiling young lady apparently was on towel collection duty. Unsure as to what to do, I stammered, 'Yes, it is.'

Seemingly oblivious to the fact that she was doing small talk with a person without clothes, she continued, 'Where are you from?'

'I go to the Bible college near here. I'm training for the ministry,' I smiled, wishing that I'd brought a waterproof Bible along if only to retain my modesty.

'Really?' she smiled. 'I'm a believer too. I go to a little evangelical church in the town.'

I now realised that I was having Christian fellowship while naked, which didn't seem quite right. Fearing that the conversation might turn into a time of worship and singing, I muttered, 'Nice to meet you,' and turned back to the face the wall. Subsequent conversations with other sweating chaps revealed that nobody blinked an eye when she came breezing through on the hunt for discarded towels. They viewed her in the same way that one might regard a medical professional. Her excursions had become the *new normal*.

Forgive me for using such an absurd illustration (even though it's totally true) to make a serious point, but here goes. Normality is constantly changing. We live in a post-modern culture, which means that we now do life without a core story as a foundation. Relativism – where truth is whatever we choose to call truth relative to us – is the quicksand upon which we build the houses of our lives. We even talk about 'my truth' and living 'your truth'. But truth isn't personalised. Something is either true or it is not.

Let's get even more serious here. In losing a core story, we have literally lost the plot. Like a football game without rules or a referee, we blunder on. Woe betide the one who suggests that there is an authentic story available, because they will be quickly dismissed as an arrogant freak, a blustering bigot.

Most of us do not experience the persecution that is felt by our brothers and sisters around the world. We worship freely, and generally are allowed to share our faith without harassment. We might wonder if outright persecution will ever arrive at our doorstep?

I think the most likely source of persecution will come because of the new normal that is increasingly ours. We will likely be able to affirm that Jesus Christ is a way to God. But when we stand with His claims to uniqueness – that He is the *only* way, truth and life – then perhaps we will hear an ominous knock of the door and a summons to suffer.

And if, and when, that new normal comes, may we be found faithful.

30 Flint, Michigan

At one point, it had the reputation of being America's most dangerous city with violent crime spiralling as a beleaguered police force fought a losing battle against drugs and guns. Flint, Michigan, is the subject of an eight-part Netflix documentary called *Flint Town*, which makes harrowing viewing. Mothers weep over the murdered bodies of their sons. Law enforcement officials openly confess their terror of going on patrol. Local politicians feud about who to blame.

It short, Flint was abandoned. Once a thriving metropolis, the hub of General Motors manufacturing with a plant so massive it was called 'Buick City', a series of economic downturns threw some knockout punches. And then a negligent engineering decision released lead into the city's water system, literally poisoning the population. The centre of the city looks like a war zone with dozens of boarded-up homes and businesses; the school buildings are closed and rotting; and there are all the associated problems that come with poverty.

My wife, Kay, and I have been to Flint on a preaching engagement. While we were there, we were invited to meet the sheriff. Images of John Wayne swaggering through the swing doors of a bar came to mind but I resisted the temptation to greet him with a 'Howdy, pardner'. With quick wit and a warm smile, Sheriff Chris organised a guided tour of the jail, which housed 630 inmates. Kay and I were then loaded into police cars and taken around the city. During the 55-minute ride, we saw a house burn down and responded to a report of a robbery that was in progress. We were dismayed as we slowly drove through the bleak streets, the sense of despair heavy in the air.

The greatest impact, however, came from the sheriff and his team. He outlined his plans for a new educational system for the jail where every inmate would be issued with an iPad – half of them were illiterate and desperately needed to learn the most basic skills. 'I'm proud of and love my city,' he said, his eyes bright. When we asked him about the source of his passion, he was emphatic. 'I became a Christian when I was 18,' he said. 'My passion and joy comes from the Holy Spirit.' That energy was infectious and was expressed by every officer we talked to. I came away from Flint with a sense that the city was not abandoned but that there are many who love it – and a lot of them are believers.

The Early Church made its mark without printing presses or social media. They were a brave lot, those first Christians, swimming against the cultural tide with their good news that Jesus, not Caesar, is Lord. They changed the world as they rolled up their sleeves, staying behind when cities were hit by plagues, caring for the dying, risking their own lives in the process. In the Roman world, something called *liberates* was practised. It was a reciprocal deal where one person would only give something to someone else provided that, later on, the favour would be returned. This arrangement worked rather well – unless you were a widow or an orphan with nothing to bring to the table. Our Christian ancestors broke with conformity and gave freely without any hope of return.

The practice of freely giving continues. Across the UK, people are quietly making a difference as they volunteer in food banks, debt counselling centres, street pastor programmes and so, so much more. Recently, I met a couple of 80-year-old ladies who don orange tabards every Saturday night to brave the streets of their city. 'We carry flip-flops and blankets with us,' one silver-haired lady said. 'The young people get so drunk in the clubs that they lose their shoes and coats, so they come out barefoot and freezing. That's where we step in, to help them stay warm and share some love and kindness in Jesus' name.'

Those ladies have also endured some sharp-tongued criticism from an unexpected source: members of their own church who feel that they are not being overtly evangelistic enough. Some have even suggested that their presence encourages excessive drinking – two criticisms that beggar belief. The delightful grey-haired warriors soldier on regardless.

Perhaps you are one of that vast army, and right now you feel tired and unappreciated. There are times when serving is the last thing you want to do. Thank you. May you know God's strength and smile as you continue the great work. And if you ever think of a city called Flint, lift a prayer because the sheriff and his posse are in town, and hope is making a comeback too.

31

No fanfare required

Fishing has never been my thing. I can't see the attraction of trudging out into the cold countryside and parking yourself in a canvas cubicle at the side of a murky river for three days. There you will sit, unwashed and therefore helpfully alone, your rod cast hopefully, feverishly anticipating the nibble of passing aquatic specimens. On the few occasions that I have ventured into fishing, I caught little, which didn't bother me because I expected little. No, fishing is not my thing.

However, fishing *was* the profession for several of Jesus' disciples. They were very good at knowing where, when and how to fish. Fishing usually took place at night in ancient Galilee, enabling fishermen to sell their catch first thing in the morning – if there was a catch, that is.

One very dark night, a huddle of exhausted, confused professional fishermen (plus a few other team members who came from other career paths) decided to fish, but there was huge disappointment in store. At the end of hours of back-breaking toil, their nets were empty. Worse still, as they neared shore, they faced the embarrassment of being quizzed by a total stranger, standing there on the beach, asking them how they'd done. 'Friends, haven't you any fish?' (John 21:5). *No, and thanks a lot for asking – pal.*

How different it would have been, had I been asked to choreograph this post-resurrection scene. I'd have hired a whole host of angels to sway on the beach and sing the 'Hallelujah' chorus from Handel's *Messiah* (prophetically, since it hadn't been composed yet). The Red Arrows would swoop overhead, billowing red and blue smoke that spelled out the words, 'Yep, He is risen!' across the sky.

The stranger was Jesus but they didn't recognise Him. This natural unassuming manner of His was consistent: in the garden on Easter morning, the one who has just triumphed in the greatest cosmic battle of history was mistaken for the gardener. Later, walking with the unhappy pair on the Emmaus Road, Jesus didn't reveal who He was and politely waited for their insistent beckoning before joining them for supper.

After following Him for a few decades, my conclusion is that God is not as obvious (or chatty, for that matter) as we sometimes depict Him. He whispers, hints and nudges, weaving prophetic riddles through dreams. At times, this makes me feel less like a disciple and more like a detective on the hunt for clues. There were those rare epic occasions in Scripture when His voice boomed and the earth shattered – occasions made into movies usually starring Charlton Heston. But they were few and far between.

Let me be frank. I wish God would speak up. I wish that,

once in a while, He would kick the door of my life in and make Himself at home. Writing that, I brace myself for some feedback, even an onslaught. Some will gently advise me that I'm not listening. They may be right. God stands at the door and knocks, not with a pounding fist, but with the lightest of taps. When His knuckles rap my door, I want to be listening and swift to answer.

Meanwhile, back on that beach, an Easter breakfast was shared. Fish and bread were served, past shame was resolved for Peter, calling was reaffirmed, and when the meal was over, their course was set to change the planet. Bewildered, overwhelmed disciples, who hadn't even been able to deliver on what they were supposed to be good at – fishing – were charged with telling the world the awesome news that death was finally done with, and everything was different.

Angels play a vital part in the unfolding fight between darkness and light. But God calls humans – tired, bleary-eyed, is-He-really-there? humans like us – to carry the Easter newsflash at a time when it's so desperately needed.

Let's look for Him, listen harder, trust when He can't be seen or heard, and share the resurrection story with words and actions in a Christ-like manner.

32
 Deciding

It was January 1945, the coldest winter in Poland in a hundred years. For prisoners held in concentration camps like Auschwitz and British soldiers in nearby prisoner-of-war camps surely it was a frozen hell. But hope jostled with terror. The distant booming of artillery announced that the liberating Russian army was coming closer, but the question on everyone's mind was: what would the Nazis do with the tens of thousands of prisoners, witnesses to their appalling crimes?

The solution was fiendishly simple – the prisoners would be forced to march; some call it the 'death march'. Many people would perish of starvation, disease or exhaustion. Those who stumbled during the 20-mile daily trudge were dispatched with a blow by a rifle butt to the neck. Any who attempted escape were shot. Trench foot and typhus were rife. Some did not change their clothes for three months, their skin teemed with lice. Food was scarce; dehydrated, they sucked on snow. Like walking dead, some soiled themselves as they shuffled along.

I learned the story of prisoner 5239. Captured at just 19, he should have been anxious about acne and girlfriends, but five long years behind barbed wire forced him to grow up fast. He was one of the thousands on the 'death march'. Suddenly, without warning, an opportunity to escape presented itself. As they rounded a bend, he glanced back and realised that the rear guard was out of sight; hurriedly looking ahead, it was the same. For ten paces or so, they would not be seen. He had a choice, a crossroad between life and death, and he decided. Turning to a friend, he hissed, 'Quick! Run! Now!'

And so, run they did, dashing into the woods. Hearts beating fast, waiting for the alarm to go up and shots to be fired, they lay on the frozen ground until at last the column passed. With no idea where they were, they finally found an isolated house. The owner, a woman whose husband was away at war, feared rape or worse. The two friends told her they meant no harm. Reassured, she cooked them a meal, and they slept in the barn. The details fade after that but, somehow, they finally made it home. He met his sweetheart, they married, and he tried to settle back into a normal life. Quizzed about those years, he said very little. Perhaps he'd decided not to give his captors any more headspace.

Hearing his story, I wanted to make a response to honour his decisiveness. And so, I have decided that I will be decisive. On that fateful day in arctic Poland, there was no time for dithering. Everything hung in the balance. And so, I want to be one who chooses well.

Every day is filled with choices, and some of them are hinges. Decisions don't call ahead or come with a health warning. While many are inconsequential, some are monumental, thinly disguised doorways to joy or tears. The Bible is crammed with life-changing decisions: Mary agrees, Peter signs up to follow, and taxman, Zacchaeus, climbs down from a tree. They chose.

And so, I will be decisive. That doesn't mean impulsive or reckless. I will be prayerful, take stock, weigh the options and consult trusted counsel. But that young man's story has nudged me to abandon meandering. I will not squander my freedom with indecision.

Many years later, that escapee made another epic choice. After decades of ignoring God, angry at the horrors he'd seen and felt, he chose to follow Christ – the greatest liberator. Shortly after, a stroke silenced his speech and he became a prisoner once more, trapped inside his own head, unable to speak an intelligible word, no means of escape. At 75 years old, he breathed his last, finally free at last.

Hearing that story, this much needs to be said: 'Thank you, prisoner 5239, for the inspiration, the legacy and the call to be decisive, brave and to take risks when the moment comes. Thank you for surviving, so that your children could exist. And thanks, most of all, for being my dad.'

Postscript: The chapter you have just read first appeared in *Christianity Magazine*. A couple of days after publication, I received an email from a reader who had read the article, and then, the next day, had found a book about a prisoner of war in a charity shop. The reader very kindly sent the book to me. What he did not know was that the book is the story of a man who was held in the same prisoner of war camp as my dad (I didn't mention the name of the camp in the article – Stalag VIII-B Lamsdorf). Today, I have a greater understanding of what my dad endured for four long years. He passed away some 25 years ago. I'm grateful to him, and to all who paid such a price in the war.

33

Awkward conversations

It was a short 15-minute bus ride from the airport car park to the terminal. A busy travel day, there were just two vacant seats, so my wife, Kay, and I squeezed ourselves into them. I was sat next to a rotund chap who was taking up more than his allotted space. Awkward.

Opposite us sat a young mum with two cute little daughters in tow, all resplendent in their *Frozen* T-shirts. Next to the smallest child was an elderly lady, her face delightfully fixed in a permanent smile. As the bus started, the smiley lady placed her hands on the little one's legs. 'I don't want you to fall off your seat when we go around corners,' she beamed. It was clear that the mum was not thrilled with this total stranger draping her arm across her daughter's lap, and the child looked like she was going to cry. This was difficult. What was surely intended as an act of care could now be interpreted as inappropriate touch, not least because the child looked mildly terrified and had likely been taught not to talk to strangers, never mind be touched by them. Awkward.

Two seats down from us sat a lady who rather obviously had a learning disability. With reduced awareness of social boundaries and a lack of inhibition, she boomed a question at the elderly smiley lady.

'WHAT'S YOUR NAME?' she hollered.

'It's Joan,' smiled the very smiley lady back. 'And what's your name?'

'MY NAME IS RUTH. DO YOU HAVE A DOG?'

Dear old Joan did indeed have a dog, no doubt a happy dog like it's owner. Ruth was delighted about this.

'I THOUGHT SO. YOU LOOK LIKE A DOG...' she paused for breath – and we all took a sharp intake of breath ourselves – 'YOU LOOK LIKE A DOG PERSON.'

Awkward.

By now, I was in agony. This was so embarrassing. I closed my eyes and wished that there was someone called Scotty who could beam me up. But there were fresh traumas to come.

'ARE YOU RELATED TO THAT LITTLE GIRL NEXT TO YOU?' enquired inquisitor Ruth.

Joan said that no, she was not.

Ruth's response boomed even louder: 'THEN WHY HAVE YOU GOT YOUR HAND ON HER LEG?'

Awkward.

As I sat there, squirming, I realised how difficult I find awkward situations. I am somewhat allergic to confrontations. When embarrassed, I announce it to the world by flushing crimson red. And many of us are the same. We don't speak up for fear of being tagged as foolish or irritating. And sometimes we Brits apologise to avoid awkward conversations. It's easy to say sorry and thus thwart the potential of a tricky exchange, and so we express regret, even sham regret.

But Jesus didn't mind awkwardness. He faced down inquisitorial Pharisees who did their best to publicly shame Him. He flew in the face of criticism by lunching with tax-collectors. Perhaps it's time to speak up, to have that difficult conversation. Some friendships remain superficial because going deeper might be uncomfortable or painful. Some churches avoid makings changes because to suggest that the current method might be failing might lead to a fall out. So things rumble on, ineffective but we don't want to risk challenging them.

At last, the bus pulled up at the terminal, and I thought our brief but excruciating excursion was ended. But I was wrong. As we got off the bus, Joan, her smile miraculously intact, decided to give Ruth a big hug. Not expecting this, Ruth just stood there, silent and ramrod straight, Joan's arms wrapped around her for what seemed like an eternity. *Really* awkward.

We did the sensible thing. We fled.

34
How to get world peace

I'm not one to boast or prone to overstate, but I do believe that a Nobel Prize is heading my way because – drumroll please – I, yes I, have found the key to world peace. With my discovery, certain world leaders will no longer be a threat (except, as I mentioned earlier, to hairdressers globally who quietly weep), politicians will actually agree about something and, miracle of miracles, might abandon acerbic tweeting. It will be achieved without an accelerating arms race, a summit of world leaders or a flurry of activity from furrow-browed diplomats. All that is required is that world leaders gather around a table not to discuss an agenda or a proposal, but to simple solve a... a jigsaw puzzle. One with at least 1,000 pieces will suffice, although an epic 10,000-piece jigsaw featuring a single panda would be even better.

I stumbled across this momentous insight during a recent Christmas family gathering that brought together people who are not used to being in close proximity. Maintaining interesting conversation from Christmas Day to Boxing Day can be hard when everyone is not used to being together for so long. It's not that there is animosity, but small talk can run dry, which can then lead to petty irritations surfacing. The pressure is heightened because the expectation for family gatherings is to have fun (especially at Christmas when everyone is expected to be gleeful *all* of the time).

Working together to build a jigsaw requires gathering in collaboration rather than competition. When the puzzle is completed, it's not that I win, but rather *we* win. We pool our efforts in the pursuit of a mutual goal. Another person sees what I don't notice and we are all the better for it. In the process of construction, sometimes painful, appreciation is shared when one person slots that elusive piece of blue sky into place.

If you don't agree with my solution to finding world peace, then consider the picture that the New Testament gives us of the Church. 'It's a jigsaw puzzle,' says Paul. Alright, he used a slightly different metaphor – the human body (perhaps because Hamleys wasn't around back them). As Paul describes the interlocking wonder that is the human body, he calls each one of us to play our part (1 Cor. 12:12–31). Spectators aren't needed, only participants. In the body, we're not uniform but called to be united; not consumers but sharers in a common kingdom vision.

As we consider recent world events, the coronavirus pandemic and unrest over the tragedy of racial injustice, it might be our mutual temptation to wonder if this fractured, broken world can ever be righted. There's no shortage of shouting, speck-hunting and planks protruding from eyes. The challenges we face seem insurmountable. But God still has a plan, and, despite our bumbling attempts, He still wants us to play our parts. The puzzle might seem to have too many pieces to ever assemble, the task might seem impossible, but we serve a God who does the impossible and sees the bigger picture on the lid of the box.

So, let's go ahead and take our places around His table. Pick up a piece. Do you know what? I think your piece belongs… right here.

Endnotes

Introduction

[1]Phillip R. Johnson, 'God without mood swings' taken from romans45.org/articles/impassib.htm [accessed July 2020]

[2]Janet Street-Porter writing for *The Independent*, 3 April 2015. To access the article, go to independent.co.uk and search for 'shouty society' [accessed July 2020]

Chapter 8: Cause and effect

[1]Stanley M. Hauerwas and William H. Willimon, *The Truth About God* (Tennessee, USA: Abingdon Press, 1999)

Chapter 11: People of the story

[1]Graham Tomlin, *The Provocative Church* (London: SPCK, 2002) p88

Chapter 13: Losing Jesus

[1]Lauren Winner, *Still* (New York, USA: HarperCollins, 2013)

Chapter 17: All grown up

[1]Eugene H. Peterson, *Working the Angles* (Michigan, USA: Eerdmans, 1993) p177

Daily Bible reading notes by Jeff Lucas

International speaker and bestselling author, Jeff Lucas, brings the Bible to life each day with these popular life application notes.

• Humour, challenge and practical insights for life
• A different topic covered in depth over two months

Find out more at **waverleyabbeyresources.org**

God's Plan for your Wellbeing

NEW book for personal use or as part of your church programme

Journey with Dave Smith through this 50-day guide, as you explore God's plan for your wellbeing. Dave also shares some of the lesson's he has learnt in order to help you, your Church, or your small group achieve the physical, emotional and spiritual balance that enables you to flourish for God and for good.

Online resources including small group discussions starters and videos available. Find out more at
waverleyabbeyresources.org/GPFYW

WAVERLEY ABBEY

Transforming lives

Waverley Abbey's vision is to enable people to experience personal transformation through applying God's Word to their lives and relationships.

Our Bible-based training and resources help people around the world to:
• Grow in their walk with God
• Understand and apply Scripture to their lives
• Resource themselves and their church
• Develop pastoral care and counselling skills
• Train for leadership
• Strengthen relationships, marriage and family life and much more.

Our insightful writers provide daily Bible reading notes and engaging resources for everyone, and our experienced course designers and presenters have gained an international reputation for excellence and effectiveness.

Our Waverley Abbey House training and conference centre in Surrey, England, provides excellent facilities in idyllic settings – ideal for both learning and spiritual refreshment.

waverleyabbey.org